Candy at Last

CANDY SPELLING

Candy at last

CANDY SPELLING

WILEY

Turner Publishing Company / Wiley General Trade
424 Church Street • Suite 2240 • Nashville, Tennessee 37219
445 Park Avenue • 9th Floor • New York, New York 10022
www.turnerpublishing.com

Candy at Last

Cover design: Maxwell Roth
Book design: Lissa Auciello-Brogan
Cover photo: © John Russo

Library of Congress Cataloging-in-Publication Data

Spelling, Candy.
 Candy at last : a memoir / Candy Spelling.
    pages cm
  ISBN 978-1-118-40950-3 (hardcover) -- ISBN 978-1-63026-072-9 (ebook)
1. Spelling, Candy. 2. Spelling, Candy--Marriage. 3. Spelling, Aaron. 4. Spelling,
Candy--Family. 5. Mothers and daughters--United States. 6. Television producers'
and directors' spouses--United States--Biography. 7. Businesswomen--United
States--Biography. 8. Women television personalities--United States--Biography. 9.
Hollywood (Los Angeles, Calif.)--Social life and customs. 10. Los Angeles (Calif.)--
Social life and customs. I. Spelling, Candy. Stories from Candyland. II. Title.
 PN1992.4.S645A3 2014
 791.4302'32092--dc23
 [B]
                        2014008604ISBN

(hardcover) 978-1-11840-950-3, ISBN (e-book) 978-1-63026-072-9

Printed in the United States of America
14 15 16 17 18 0 9 8 7 6 5 4 3 2 1

FOREVER AARON
who is the heart and soul of who I am today

Contents

x   Contents

Foreword

We were sitting in the living room of Candy Spelling's famous (actually, legendary) home in Beverly Hills. We had always wanted to get a tour of the house ever since we met Aaron and Candy at a dinner party at the home of Marvin and Barbara Davis while we were on the Oscar circuit of dinners in 2002 for our movie *Chicago*. But time passed; Aaron was no longer with us. But one day we got a call from Candy—out of the blue—asking if we'd come over one afternoon for coffee.

We knew quite a bit about Candy from all the many stories of her philanthropy, her generosity of spirit, and her beloved, sparkling wit and charm. But nothing prepared us for that wonderful afternoon at the Manor (second to no place on earth other than the Dynasty Mansion or Downton Abbey).

We arrived and we were excited to be guided through the long-awaited tour. Afterward (back in the living room) we reminisced about Aaron and his staggering accomplishments, and we, first and foremost, witnessed a vital and energetic woman who was ready to begin the next chapter of her life. But what could that possibly be?

We perceived that Candy had learned much from Aaron's business smarts, but she also knew a lot about the life and world of a producer.

Although we arrived with no agenda, we suddenly blurted out: "Have you ever thought of becoming a Broadway producer?"

She seemed surprised. Kind of shocked. But instantly intrigued.

Not long afterward, after many other meetings and phone calls, Candy found herself listed up there with the other co-producers of our two upcoming productions: *Promises, Promises* starring Sean Hayes and Kristin Chenoweth and *How to Succeed in Business Without Really Trying* starring Daniel Radcliffe and John Larroquette, two Tony-winning hits. (She subsequently continued her Broadway producing without us, helping mount *Nice Work If You Can Get It* and *After Midnight*.)

We learned a lot about Candy during our New York adventures. She was a born producer. Great instincts. A sense of fearlessness. Amazing taste. And a keen understanding of marketing, publicity, and merchandising. She was savvy and had a laser-beam ability to find problems and solve them. We were so grateful to have her on our team.

But we also got to know Candy the person. Warm, kind, and damn funny. Her wit kept us laughing—and on our toes. You couldn't hope for a greater friend. Or partner.

We got to know Candy Spelling 2.0. And we feel so fortunate to have her in our lives.

And whether it was from keen observation or pure osmosis from her earlier years, we launched a new producer. Aaron would have been so proud.

As proud of her as we are today.

—Craig Zadan and Neil Meron

Preface

I 've lived my life in three different stages. There were my formative years, growing up with my family. Then I was an ingénue who dated and later married the hardest-working television writer in Hollywood. Aaron's world of famous faces and sophistication was an intimidating milieu, especially for a shy young woman who was raised to speak only when spoken to. Fortunately for me, my new husband's talents at the typewriter were matched by his kindness and generous spirit. With his loving support, I was able to overcome these emotional obstacles and fill the shoes his immense success laid out for me.

Despite having a very public profile, our family life was very private. Aaron and I didn't go out at night. We weren't seen anywhere cool. We did things like take the kids to Swenson's Ice Cream Parlor. We also liked to have our closest friends over for movie night in our home. In fact, it was only about seven years ago that I went to my first concert to see Madonna.

Until recently, I never spoke publicly or gave any interviews. I suppose this is why it has been so easy for me to be characterized as the cunning Alexis Carrington. The truth is, I am more like Blake's dutiful wife, Krystle Carrington, but let's face it—she wasn't very exciting.

For almost four decades, my job was to create the stable home life Aaron needed so he could be out there in the Hollywood trenches. When he became ill, we had a complete role reversal. I had to step up and take over. Protecting Aaron from scrutiny and preserving his reputation became my number-one priority.

When Aaron died, I not only lost my partner in life. I was also suddenly missing the force of nature who had defined me and our family. For the first time in thirty-eight years, I had to learn to function in the big, scary world on my own. There were new challenges every day and I was definitely out of my comfort zone.

When I sat down to share my story, my intention was to share the beginning of my life with Aaron Spelling. Then I thought about the absolutely amazing letters I receive from women who have been recently widowed or who have terminally ill husbands. They share their grief and fears with me, or tell me that something I said gave them strength. I had never thought about how my personal experiences might help other women. Once I realized I could have a positive impact, I decided it was time to talk about the end of Aaron's life as well.

With age has also come the loss of my filters. So before I knew it, I was writing about my misadventures of dating and sex. After forty years of being with the same partner, it was a whole new world. This is uncharted territory for a woman of my age, and I am certain the media will have at it. But honestly, I don't think they could possibly say anything worse about me than they already have.

Over the years, I have learned the difference between things that I can change and things that will always be the same. With the help of some very good therapy, I have resolved my own internal feelings about my complex relationship with my daughter, and here, for the first time, I am able to write honestly about it.

It's been a few months now since I turned my completed manuscript into my publisher. Reading over the chapters, I am very proud of my work and the insights I impart. Despite all of my ups and downs, there is very little I would go back and change in my life. Even during the toughest times when there was a giant elephant in the room, there was a life lesson to be learned.

There is an old adage that asks, "How do you deal with an elephant in the room?" The answer to this has proved true time and again, "You deal with it one bite at a time."

Introduction

The air on the second floor of the mortuary definitely seemed thinner than it had been in the lobby downstairs. I was cold and having trouble breathing. The melancholic energy hit me like an invisible force field as soon as I stepped off the elevator. I tried to make polite eye contact with the somber funeral arranger as he stepped aside so I could make the left-hand turn down the hallway to the room where the coffins were displayed. The more steps we took, the longer the hallway seemed to grow. I thought we would never get there. Choosing the coffin and the liner would be the conclusion of almost an entire day spent at the cemetery making decisions for the last place on Earth my husband would be.

It was a sunny day in mid-June. Normally in Los Angeles we have June gloom all month, but on this day, the sun was out. The warm weather made walking the entire grounds that much more taxing. I had brought my twenty-eight-year-old son Randy for moral support, thinking we could make decisions together, but he was understandably having trouble coping. Aaron was still alive but slipping away every day. I was just a few years older than Randy was when my mother died. I had learned from this experience that it was better to take care of these arrangements in a relatively stable state of mind. My father completely fell apart, and it was all left on my shoulders.

Randy ran out of the room as I struggled to make a decision on the color of the satin liner. He probably thought I was going on and on about things that didn't matter, but Randy wasn't a husband yet. He didn't understand the weight of these decisions. This would be the last thing I would do for my husband of thirty-eight years. It didn't matter that nobody would see Aaron; I wanted to put the same care and attention to detail in these decisions that I had throughout our marriage. I wanted it to be perfect for him. It was no different from making sure his shirts were neatly folded and put away. Or the way I always had his favorite snacks laid out precisely the way he liked them when he sat down in front of the television to watch football. Aaron, I knew, would have expected me to handle it just this way.

I let Randy run outside without going after him. He was better off waiting for me in the car. I stayed and finished my business because it had to be done, and it was my job to do it.

Candy at last

1

The Torn Ribbon on My Heart

Aaron had been living in a prison for the last two years. He had suffered a stroke and been diagnosed with Alzheimer's disease. Alzheimer's is a scary and mysterious disease, but my mourning didn't begin on the day of his diagnosis. It began when he refused to get out of bed and refused to be nourished. His doctor came to the house regularly to check on him and hydrate him intravenously. The doctor wanted to take him down the street to UCLA Medical Center where he could be managed more completely, but Aaron was very clear.

"No thanks, Doc."

"You don't really want to be here, do you?

"That's right, Doc."

My husband didn't want to be sustained knowing he couldn't live the life he knew and loved. I watched him waste away. He got so thin that his wedding band would slide off his finger. His nurse and I convinced him to leave it on his bed table so he wouldn't panic when it slipped off and he couldn't find it.

There was at least a good year when Aaron couldn't go out with me. Some of our most thoughtful friends got me out of the house for lunches and dinners. After a while I started getting uncomfortable because it was the same friends constantly taking me out. Normally I would have reciprocated by having them for dinner at the house, but Aaron was in bad shape, and I knew he wouldn't want anyone to see him in this condition. I didn't even feel comfortable inviting people over.

I decided I could remedy this by joining Hillcrest Country Club. They had Sunday night barbecues and al fresco dining with music on Friday nights. I would be able to invite other couples, and they wouldn't be able to pick up the check. Only members are allowed to pay for food and drinks at country clubs. As a member, I would just sign a chit and then get a monthly bill in the mail. Problem solved.

A woman joining a country club on her own is a bold move. Hillcrest was a men's club right up until the 1980s, when the by-laws were changed. Prior to that, women were allowed there only if their husbands were members, and if the husband died, the membership could only be passed to a son. Instead of calling this chauvinism, they called it "legacy." Not surprisingly, there was not one woman on the review board. Just a tribunal of twelve men asking me why I was joining the club as a single woman and not with my husband.

Their memories were obviously short and the administration files not very comprehensive. Aaron had been a member over a decade ago. He only joined at the insistence of Marvin Davis, who was head of 20th Century Fox Studios at the time. The truth was, Aaron was usually working, and when he wasn't, his favorite pastime was sitting around the table with the kids laughing and eating. We had our own tennis court at home, so we never went to the club. Well, one day the membership committee showed up at our old house on South Mapleton Drive to complain that Aaron wasn't using his membership enough. Aaron may have been mild-mannered, but he never liked being told what to do. He very politely suggested they refund him his $50,000 membership fee and in turn, he wouldn't be a member there anymore. When we closed the door on our visitors that night, he said, "They can take their membership and . . ."

Instead of reminding the board of this episode, I mustered my courage and told them the truth. "If you don't already know, my husband is very ill and is going to die. If I join with him, then you're just going to make me do this all over again because the membership will belong to him or my son."

The men all got very quiet after I spoke. I don't think they knew quite what to say since I had been so truthful and to the point. They had nothing to argue with me about. Ultimately, I turned out to be the third woman to be given membership on her own.

At this point Aaron needed medical care twenty-four hours a day, seven days a week. The thermostat in the master bedroom was turned up to seventy-six degrees, and still he lay there under two duvets, freezing. I had moved into Tori's old room so Aaron would be more comfortable and the nurses could look after his needs. I would go sit with him in what used to be our room. It felt foreign. Nothing was the same anymore.

Sherreth was one of Aaron's nurses who is still my friend to this day. She was so sweet, soulful, and compassionate. There were days when Aaron would be really angry with me when I got home after being out for just a few hours. Sometimes I went to therapy, which I needed desperately, and other times I would just go out for long drives to give myself space and clear my head. I understood that often with dementia, people get crabby. I knew the fighting was coming from his confused mind, but it was still tough especially because he had never spoken to me this way in all the years that we were married. Sherreth would always step in and say, "Mr. Spelling, you've been waiting for your wife to come home, and now she's home and you pick a fight with her."

Aaron's clear moments became fewer and far between. Strangely, at the end, he was very clear. I should have known that was the day he was going to die. That morning, Sherreth encouraged me to go to the hairdresser. She promised, as always, that she would call and give me a heads up if she thought the time was coming. Well, when her call came through on my cell, I knew before I even answered, it was real. I literally ran out of the salon in West Hollywood with my hair soaking wet. I had driven myself and as I raced home, West Hollywood seemed light-years away from The Manor.

I made it home in time and climbed into bed with my husband. I held him in my arms and tried to comfort him. I kept saying, "I'm here. I'm right here." Sherreth had explained there would be a death chant as the body shut down and the last of the oxygen was expelled from Aaron's lungs. It was unbelievably excruciating and it seemed to go on forever. Finally, Aaron took his last breath, and he was gone. I held onto him and wailed like a child. After what must have been a few hours, Sherreth took him out of my arms.

On the day of his burial, I went to view his body. I honestly can't remember if Randy went with me. He may have but he didn't go into the room with me to see Aaron, and that was okay. I couldn't help but think they had done his hair wrong and I wished I had brought him one of his older shirts that would have fit his fragile frame better. I took a mental picture of him, one I'll never forget, and then they pulled down the lid. It was easier for me once the coffin was closed. We had a small service of about thirty or forty people, just family and close friends. I chose a sarcophagus inside the hilltop mausoleum as Aaron's final resting place. I wanted him to be above ground, and I wanted his grave to reflect his magnificent character, his incredible accomplishments, and his brilliance.

One of my clearest and most moving memories from that day was when Tori, Randy, and I lined up before the service for the tearing of the ribbon. It's a very touching Jewish mourning tradition rooted in the biblical stories of David, Jacob, and Job, all of whom tore their clothes when they received tragic news. The ribbon is pinned to the clothes of the bereaved, usually right over the heart, then torn by the rabbi.

After the burial, we retreated to The Manor. I had organized some very simple catering. I remember thinking, what is it with funerals and food? The last thing I wanted to do was eat. The reception was endless and uncomfortable, yet I dreaded the thought of being alone that night. The house had already taken on a different countenance. I realized that day the importance of letting people take care of you in times like these. So when my dear friend Willy offered to spend the night with me and stay for a few nights, I took her up on it.

I definitely didn't laugh about it then, but I do now. Because I am who I am, nobody came to the door with any homemade casseroles. There was only one platter of food delivered to the house. It was a deli platter sent courtesy of Hillcrest Country Club.

2

Beverly Hills Child Bride

It was 1964 and I was probably the only teenage girl who hadn't been infected with the Beatlemania epidemic. When The Beatles came to Los Angeles, one of my girlfriends found out where they were staying and paid for a helicopter to airlift her into the backyard of the house. At nineteen, I was an old soul in a young body. I loved classic jazz and music from the 1940s. I was also wiser beyond my years having already been married and divorced.

I was only seventeen when I married my boyfriend, Howard, who was twenty-one at the time. Like most girls that age, I didn't know who I was yet or what I wanted from life, but I bought into the fairy tale when Howard proposed. My family lived in Beverly Hills, which, in the post–World War II years, was being shaped as a glamorous shopping and lifestyle destination. The city's famous hotels like the iconic pink Beverly Hills Hotel and the Beverly Wilshire Hotel, which had just been renovated to include a ballroom for big bands, brought tourists from all over the world. Funny enough, I think it was *The Jack Benny Show,* which used Beverly Hills as a backdrop, that put the fabled city on the map of America's imagination.

My parents were regular middle-class people living beyond their means. Of course my father, Merritt Marer, was the only one who knew this very privileged information. He was a traveling salesman for a furniture line. My mother, Augusta Gene Marer, who later changed her name legally to Gene, was a beautiful woman consumed with all things elegant. She was a fit model for dress companies and an absolute perfectionist. We had a houseman named Taylor who drove my brother, Tony, and me to school. His wife, Lena, was our housekeeper.

Being driven to kindergarten by a chauffeur is not all that it is cracked up to be. In fact, it was awful. Children don't want to be singled out at school, and I was no exception, so I had Taylor drop me off two blocks away from the school so I could walk just like all the other five-year-olds. Probably not unlike other families of this generation, my brother and I didn't speak unless spoken to, and decisions were made for us without any discussion. This included what I wore to school. While everyone else was wearing blue Oxfords with white-striped laces, I was in fancy black patent leather Mary Janes. My clothes were always a fancier style than what everyone else was wearing, and I was bullied. Even the other mothers phoned my mother to ask why I wore such expensive clothes to school. What they didn't know was that we didn't shop at Saks or Magnins. We shopped at moderately priced stores like Lerners. My clothes were not actually expensive, they just looked expensive.

Ultimately it didn't matter, I suppose. At the end of the day, I just didn't fit in with the other kids. All the teasing devastated me, and I was held back from moving on to the first grade. In the teacher's assessment, I was not emotionally mature enough for the next grade. Needless to say, flunking kindergarten did not do wonders for my self-esteem, and, sadly, from that time on I think my mother held the belief that I was not very smart.

About this time my father suffered some financial missteps when he expanded his retail furniture business too quickly. We lost everything including our home and were forced to move into an apartment in Hollywood. Ironically, what was ruinous to my parents financially was a blessing to my childhood development. We could no longer afford to keep Taylor, so now I walked two miles to the bus stop and then used public transportation to get to school every day. I really enjoyed being out in the world and getting a taste of real life. My new school was also significantly less competitive, and I was able to skip a grade and make up for having been held back.

Despite our circumstances, my mother continued my "proper" upbringing. I learned how to cook and set a French table service, which my mother still set every night for our family dinner. I also learned the art of needlepoint, was taught to entertain, and even went to private school where among other social graces I learned to curtsy.

Like all daughters, I wanted to be perfect for my mother. I was thrilled when I pleased her by meeting her demands. Unfortunately, there was another side to this. When I failed to live up to her high expectations, I could see that she felt that *she* had failed. This was extremely difficult for me and undermined my self-confidence in the most damaging way. I was already shy, and this made me even more so. I also had trouble making eye contact with people, and I absolutely dreaded making conversation with strangers.

We eventually recovered enough financially that we could return to Beverly Hills. I was a student at Beverly Hills High School when I met Howard. Our courtship was typical of high-school romances; we parked our car and necked, stopped at Dolores's Coffee Shop on La Cienega for burgers and Cherry Lime Rickeys. We were crazy about each other, and fortunately for my mother, Howard wasn't just my type—he was also hers. His family was wealthy, they owned a very successful transport business, and Howard himself owned a ski shop in Beverly Hills. Despite being disappointed in the size of the diamond in my engagement ring, my mother gave us her blessing, and we embarked on planning our wedding.

My parents were not in any position to pay for the lavish wedding my mother envisioned, and I really didn't want them to spend money they didn't have, so we took the advice of Howard's mother and eloped to Las Vegas. Because I was still a minor, my parents came to Las Vegas with us. We had a very sweet ceremony at the Flamingo Hotel. It was a very happy day for everyone.

Howard and I took a two-and-a-half-weeklong Mariposa cruise to Hawaii for our honeymoon. At the time they were one of the premium cruise operators, so when we got back, everyone wanted to hear all the wonderful details of our luxurious trip. The detail that was at the forefront of my mind, but the one I did not want to discuss (eventually I had to tell my mother), was the fact that somehow I had returned from my honeymoon still a virgin.

So in addition to being set up in a 2,000-square-foot apartment on Oakhurst Drive, I was also taken to the gynecologist for my very first pelvic examination. The discomfort of the exam was one thing, and then there was the humiliation of the doctor's conversation with me and my mother. It was so strange that suddenly my body, not to mention my sex life, was everybody's business. At the end of the day, I was given a clean bill of health. The doctor's conclusion was simply that I was very young and stressed out about my "first time."

Eventually Howard and I would consummate our relationship, but our intimacy issues, which continued, were the least of our problems. Now that we were man and wife and spending our days together, I saw firsthand that Howard had absolutely no work ethic. I spent more time at the ski shop than he did. Howard preferred spending his days at a casino in Gardena playing poker. We were well provided for by his parents, but we were still expected to speak only when spoken to, even though we were a young married couple.

I still remember when my father-in-law called to tell me that he had purchased us a refrigerator. I asked if I could see it or choose the color before it was delivered, and he told me that I couldn't. Instead, he gave me instructions to be home for the delivery. On another occasion, he drove me out to look at a house he was buying for us. It was not the "starter" home I was expecting. It was a five-bedroom family home, and he made it very clear those rooms were to be filled with grandchildren.

That, I think, is when Howard and I truly fell apart. There was a lot of pressure to have children, and up until that point, Howard and I had only had sex maybe eight times. I also started to feel like Howard's father was my husband and not my father-in-law. I didn't have the emotional vocabulary yet to express how I was feeling. I wasn't completely unhappy, but I also knew I wasn't happy. I couldn't talk about how I was feeling with my mother. We just didn't talk about those things. To his credit, my father initiated several conversations with me in which he told me it was okay to admit I had made a mistake and that my marriage wasn't working. But I held on, fearful that if I couldn't make this work, it meant there was something wrong with me.

They say that sometimes God does for you what you can't do for yourself. One night after another fight, Howard walked out on our marriage. I was so scared and even more frightened of telling my parents. It turned out Howard had already called my parents to tell them he had left and that I was alone at the apartment. I'll never forget my father saying they were coming to get me. Hearing those words made my heart skip a beat. I felt so embarrassed.

My mother was not a nurturing person, but she definitely had a "take-charge" personality. Her way of mothering me during this crisis was to rescue me. She had me and all of the furniture they had given us packed up and out of the apartment in record time. And in the best way she could, she did try to talk me through what was happening.

Three weeks after I filed for divorce from Howard, I received a phone call from Howard's family physician. He asked me to come meet with him at his office. I wasn't sure what this was all about, but I went in anyway. The doctor's line of questioning was very personal, and I confided in him about our intimacy issues. He listened very carefully and then offered his professional opinion that it was unclear whether Howard preferred women or men. The bottom line for the doctor was that the United States was drafting men to fight in the Vietnam War, so I needed to reconcile with him to decrease his chances of being called to service.

The doctor's mandate made me feel as if I were living in the dark ages and had no rights. I was not a possession and had no intention of going back to Howard so I could be his Draft Lottery "Beard." I followed through with the divorce proceedings, and months later we finally had our day in court. I petitioned to have my name legally changed back to Marer, and Howard petitioned to keep the monogrammed poker chips my mother had given him as a wedding gift.

3

Caught in Aaron's Spell

One of my all-time favorite movie quotes is from *Hannah and Her Sisters*. It's at the very end of the film when Woody Allen's hypochondriac character, Mickey, has found love again (with his ex-wife's sister, no less). "The heart is a very, very, resilient little muscle. It really is," he says to his former sister-in-law, who has turned out to be his soulmate.

Living back at home with my parents, I found this to be true. Possibly even more so since I was still so young. For a while I felt like nobody would ever want to date me again, but I really didn't have any trouble getting dates. I also had lots of good conversations with my mother, and that helped me to move on as well. One afternoon, Jack Hanson, former shortstop for the Los Angeles Angels, stopped me on the street. It was Nancy Sinatra Jr. who best described Jack when she said, "My father, Hugh Hefner, and Jack Hanson are the three most important men in America." Jack and his designer wife, Sally, had made a fortune with their signature "hip-slim pants." Jackie Kennedy, Audrey Hepburn, Marlene Dietrich, and Marilyn Monroe were just a few of the celebrities who wore his cute clothes. His exclusive stores, called Jax, were in New York, Chicago, San Francisco, Palm Beach, and South Hampton. His flagship store was in Beverly Hills. Jack offered me a job there. I told him I had never worked in a retail store and that I could only work four hours a day, but he gave me the job anyway.

I was being paid on commission, so I instinctively knew that having the right attitude was going to be the key to succeeding at the store. Boy, was I right. All of the other girls, who, like me, were hired for their looks, were incredibly lazy. They were all dressed up and made up, but they couldn't seem to get up and out of their chairs to help the customers. I was adamant about being nice to customers regardless of how they treated me. I was also very industrious and didn't make a big deal of bringing up the clothes from the back. The result was that in just four hours, I made more than most girls did working eight.

Jack also happened to be the owner of the Daisy, a private nightclub and discotheque on Beverly Drive. It was the kind of place where everyone who was anyone went to be seen and have a good time. In 1967, Dan Jenkins of *Sports Illustrated* wrote, "Every night and most every day in the technicolor life of a man named Jack Hanson it rains dream girls. They pour down from the heaven of Beverly Hills with those exquisite faces, luscious figures, and that long, serious hair the color of ravens or oranges or sunlight. They are actresses and starlets, dancers and models, heiresses and conveniences, and Jack Hanson relishes them all—every slinking, shiny, unimpoverished one. He sees them in the evenings, either Twiggy-eyed or smoldering, at his brutally private club, the Daisy."

The doors to the club were open to all of the girls who worked at the store. Even though Jack probably let my co-workers and me in as eye candy, it still felt very special to be there. Paul Newman, Steve McQueen, Katharine Ross, and Peter Sellers were just a few of the stars referred to as "Jax Pack."

One weekend while my parents were out of town, I stayed over at my girl-friend Ronnie's house. Ronnie had a date on Saturday night and was pressuring me to double with her date and his friend Lee. I really wasn't interested in

Lee, but as much as I liked Ronnie's mother, I didn't want to spend my Saturday night at home with her. So double date it was.

We started the evening with dinner at La Scala and of course wound up at the Daisy later that night. As usual, the club was a scene. Tina Sinatra was there with songwriter Wes Farrell, who was riding high on the success of his number-one single, "Hang On Sloopy." Lee was friendly with both of them, so we sat with them at their table.

Aaron was also in attendance that night with a date on his arm. I knew all about him from the gossip at the store. It was a real "who's who" in there during business hours. Aaron was a television writer at Four Star Entertainment, the production company behind shows like *The Big Valley, Burke's Law,* and *The June Allyson Show.*

Aaron was also known as a charming playboy around town. He was seen out with a different starlet or model every night. On this night, his date looked annoyed that he kept stopping by our table to whisper into Tina's ear. I had no idea what he was saying to her. Finally, he asked me to dance.

There was something indescribable between us from the moment we met. It was a profound connection. New Agers might say we had shared a past life. Psychologists would probably say it was all projection. Cynics would say it was lust. Call it what you will, it was real. I remember feeling like we could see something in each other that no one else could. I think we danced to eight or nine songs together, including "My Funny Valentine." During one of the dances, Aaron said, "I'm going to marry you some day." It was an eye-rolling moment for me. I thought, *Oh yeah, what a line! I mean really, what a line!* When I got back to my table, Lee was standing there holding my coat open for me. Our date was clearly over. I have no idea what happened to Aaron's date, and I never asked him.

On our way out of the club, Ronnie told Aaron that I was staying with her. He gave Ronnie his number and made her promise that I would call him. I made a detour to my house for a change of clothes before returning to Ronnie's. As soon as I walked in, she handed me Aaron's number and insisted I call him. When I refused, she dialed Aaron's number and practically forced me to take the receiver. He was very happy to hear from me, and we talked until five in the morning. Despite Aaron being a terrific "phone date," I was all too aware of his reputation. I knew all about the starlets on the sets and what went on once the cameras had wrapped. As smitten as we both were, I didn't want to be his flavor of the week. I determined that I would not get caught up with Aaron.

The next morning came around fast since I had been up all night. I was bleary eyed when Ronnie's mom burst into the bedroom and said we were taking a spontaneous trip to Las Vegas to meet Ronnie's father there. We got so caught up in the excitement that we forgot we didn't have a ride to the airport. I'm not sure what got into me, but even though I hadn't hung up the phone all that long ago, I called Aaron and asked him if he would drive us to the airport. I did my best to sound very cavalier to cover up how much I already liked him.

As for Aaron, he was happy to oblige on the condition that when we returned on Sunday afternoon, I would agree to play hostess at the barbecue he had at his house every Sunday evening. When he met us at the airport on Sunday, he presented me with a little gold pin in the shape of a rose with two little leaves made of rubies and emeralds. There was a diamond on the rose. I told him I couldn't accept it, but he insisted and so I did. I was still a little suspicious of Mr. Spelling and his casting couch. Maybe he was a fast mover and this was part of his repertoire? I couldn't be sure, so I chose to believe this was something special he had done for me.

4

The Writing on the Wall

y mother was fit to be tied when she returned from her long weekend and heard about how I had spent mine. In fairness, Aaron was twenty three years older than me, I had met him at a nightclub, and after knowing him for less than two days, I had gone to his house to play hostess for his weekly Sunday night dinner gathering. She was also convinced he had a sock drawer full of those Raymond & Company Jewelers pins. For her, the writing was on the wall.

"Why are you dating Aaron Spelling when Del Coleman is crazy about you?" Del Coleman was someone I'd had a few dates with. He owned a vending machine company and was quite handsome. We'd been out a few times, but I just wasn't into him.

True to her eighteenth-century sensibilities, for my mother it always came down to finances, and she was ever determined to find me a marital situation in which I would be taken care of. When I met Aaron, he was not yet Aaron Spelling as we would come to know him. He had just left an enviable staff writing position to set up his own shingle with Danny Thomas. It was a huge risk and an unprecedented move at the time for a television writer. Aaron was completely without pretension. In fact, he made no bones about scrounging around Desilu Productions for office furniture he could use in his empty office. His vision and drive were intoxicating. He was unlike anyone I had ever met.

Despite our completely different upbringings, we actually had a lot in common. Aaron understood my confidence issues. He had grown up poor in Dallas, Texas, where his only opportunity to watch television was through the window of a local appliance store. On the way to school, he had to watch out for a group of boys who would beat him up and take his shoes. He had to finish his walk to school without them and arrived to the schoolyard barefoot and humiliated. The saddest story Aaron ever told me was when he won a shiny red bicycle from a store called Sanger Brothers. It was a poetry contest, and he won fair and square, but the store owners refused to give him the bike because he was Jewish.

Even before Aaron had given me this glimpse into his childhood, I felt I could be vulnerable with him. On our third or fourth date, we spent the whole night practicing my social skills. Aaron was, of course, the master. He could talk to anyone. It didn't matter whether it was a busboy at a restaurant or a prince, he could have an interesting conversation that made the other person feel good about themselves. So Aaron coached me on making eye contact, shaking hands, and stirring up polite dinner conversation with strangers. It sounds like an odd way to spend an evening, but it helped me and it meant a lot to me that Aaron believed in me.

Another commonality between us was that we both had first marriages that hadn't worked out. Aaron was thirty years old when he came to Los Angeles in 1953 on borrowed money. He didn't have a car or even a type-writer. Just his ideas and his work ethic, which he quickly to put to use working as a roadie of sorts for an all-woman orchestra known as the Ada Leonard Orchestra. Aaron was also working on developing his writing at the Actors Studio in Hollywood. It was there that he met actress Carolyn Jones, who was a fellow Texan.

For a pair of struggling creative types, one rent payment was better than two, but they both had their sense of Texas propriety. So instead of just "shackin' up," Aaron and Carolyn were married. Not unlike my own young marriage, Aaron quickly became disillusioned once he was living with Carolyn. He came home every evening to find his wife intoxicated. The smell of alcohol filled their home and was all over their things. Even though she was earning recognition as an actress, including an Academy Award nomination for Best Supporting Actress in Paddy Chayefsky's 1957 film *The Bachelor Party* as well as a Golden Globe Award for Most Promising Newcomer, Carolyn remained emotionally unstable. Being the caretaker that Aaron was, he was determined to honor his commitment to the "worse" of "for better or worse" in his marriage vows.

Aaron and Carolyn were known for entertaining, and the guest list to their parties was like the list of invitees to a Hollywood premiere. It was what went on in the house when nobody was around that was so difficult. The straw that broke the camel's back came twelve years into their marriage when Carolyn tried to shoot herself in the bathtub at their house on Beverly Drive. Aaron felt awful for calling it quits but followed through with the divorce. His Jewish guilt got the better of him, so he remained friendly with her afterward. We even went to a few cocktail parties at her house when we were dating. It was more than a little bit awkward, but I did it for Aaron.

I sometimes wondered if his bathtub story was all true. Going to her parties, I had the opportunity to see how sweet she was when she was sober and then how caustic and destructive she became after a couple of drinks. I think Aaron was able to resolve his feelings about their relationship after he helped her land the role of a lifetime playing Morticia Addams in *The Addams Family*.

5

Our Comedy of Manners

Aaron shot the pilot of *The Mod Squad* for ABC shortly after we started dating. His inspiration for what became known as the "hippie cop show" was a conversation he had with Bud Ruskin, a retired policeman whom he met at the Daisy. The policeman told Aaron that law enforcement was recruiting young people for undercover police work, and this set Aaron's mind alight. Aaron pitched his idea for the show to his business partner, Danny Thomas, who promptly told him he was out of his mind. Danny quickly added that Aaron should "go for it." Unbeknownst to Aaron, he was about to change the landscape of prime-time television with his youth market formulation.

Aaron and I dated each other exclusively over the next two and a half years. We had very glamorous dates, and other times we were like a pair of teenagers. Before Aaron dropped me off at home for the evening at my parents', we'd park the car at a little park off Doheny Drive and Carmelita Avenue in Beverly Hills. We, along with Aaron's 120-pound Belgian shepherd, Adam, would steam up the windows of his black Cadillac Brougham. It was a chic car to have, and it had a special bench row in the front. The funny thing about the car was that it had these two massive car phones in it. One in the front and another in the back. I never understood why Aaron had a phone in the back since he didn't have a driver.

Herald-Express gossip columnist Harrison Carroll, who was a fixture of the Hollywood scene, wrote about us several times. First I was the flavor of the week, and then I was the flavor of *every* week. I used to cut out and save every column that mentioned us. It was fun for me until Carroll wrote, "At the Daisy Club, I asked Producer Aaron Spelling if he and Candy Marer have any wedding plans. 'Not yet,' he replied, 'but I really want to.' Don't know if it had anything to do with this admission but Aaron promptly got the hiccups. And tried what was, to me, a novel cure. Drinking water out of a paper cup covered with a tissue."

It definitely wasn't smooth sailing. We had two breakups and a marriage proposal in between. We had actually gone to city hall and gotten a marriage license, but Aaron let it expire. I knew that however unconscious it may have been for him, his hesitation had to do with Carolyn. I think he had anxiety about being trapped in a bad marriage again, and I also believe he was still trying to protect her feelings. It was very hurtful for me.

Our breakup times were miserable, especially when I ran into Aaron while he was out on a date or vice versa. Right around this time my father told me it was time for me to get my own apartment, because waiting up for me until the wee hours was negatively impacting my mother's health. I was very surprised, because in those days nice Jewish girls didn't live on their own. I decided I would take a big step and move across the country to New York City and try my hand at modeling. My mother did not agree with my proposed move to Manhattan. She felt I was trying to force Aaron to marry me. What my mother clearly did not understand about Aaron was that nobody could force him to do anything he didn't want to do.

My mother found a residence hotel for women called the Barbizon Hotel. It was located on the Upper East Side and was known as a safe hotel for women traveling alone to New York City for professional opportunities. The hotel didn't allow men above the ground floor, and it observed strict dress and conduct codes. The hotel had a library, a lounge where all the residents watched television and played games. There was even an indoor swimming pool. Lauren Bacall, Grace Kelly, Joan Didion, and Candice Bergen were just of few of the hotel's past famous residents. It sounded perfect. In his 2010 *Vanity Fair* article "Sorority on E. 63rd St.," Michael Callahan wrote, "According to a writer for *Time* magazine, it was 'one of the few places in Gomorrah-on-the-Hudson where a girl could take her virtue to bed and rest assured it would still be there next morning.' What's more, the building possessed 'the greatest concentration of beauty east of Hollywood.'"

Even though I was from Los Angeles, I still felt like a girl from a small town going to the big city for her first time. I had never been to New York City before. I immediately loved the energy and the sophistication. I was so excited to get to the hotel and start my new life as a "Barbizon Girl." After hearing that Grace Kelly had danced in the halls of the Barbizon in her underwear, I guess my expectation was that the hotel would look like a beautiful set from *High Society*. Well, I couldn't have been more wrong. The rooms were so small they were claustrophobic. There was a narrow single bed pushed up against a wall and a writing desk an arm's length away against the other side of the room. The mix of Gothic, Romanesque, and Renaissance-style architecture created hallways that were gloomy and depressing. My room was more convent cell than sorority dormitory, and it goes without saying I didn't feel like breaking into song in my underwear.

I left Los Angeles on good terms with Aaron. We were still very close and spoke on the phone almost every day. I was getting work as a model and was determined to stick it out at the Barbizon until I could rent an apartment. One day while we were on the phone, Aaron talked me into spending a romantic weekend with him. Since he didn't fly, I booked a flight home and he reserved a suite for us at the Bel-Air hotel. The only glitch in our spontaneous plan was that I was supposed to have a blind date with the son of a couple my parents were friendly with. I didn't know much about him, only that he was a stockbroker. When Aaron invited me out to Los Angeles, I didn't think twice about canceling the blind date. Without any remorse whatsoever, I left a message with the stockbroker's secretary.

Hours later, Aaron met me at the airport in Los Angeles. I was elated to be with him, and we went straight to our suite at the Bel-Air hotel. It was incredibly romantic—at least until the phone started ringing off the hook, that is. Aaron finally answered the phone. It was his assistant, Shelley. She told Aaron that my mother had called the office hysterical because I had gone missing in New York City. Apparently, for whatever reason, the stockbroker in New York had called me back at the Barbizon, and when he couldn't reach me, he called his parents in Los Angeles. After hanging up with their son, the stockbroker's parents immediately called my mother, who then called Shelley. She told Shelley that if I had gone missing, she knew for certain that Aaron knew where I was.

There was no caller ID back then, so I could have easily called my mother back and told her a fib. Instead, I panicked. I threw all of my clothes, which were only sexy nightgowns, by the way, back into the suitcase and had Aaron drive me straight back to the airport. Don't ask me what my thought process was, but I got on the next flight to New York City and called her as soon as I landed. My mother didn't even give me chance to start in on the story I had concocted. She immediately hung up on me. I called her back a second time and launched in on my lie, but before I could finish, she hung up on me a second time.

Shortly after the "incident," I moved out of the Barbizon and into an L-shaped apartment on 53rd Street between First and Second Avenues. It wasn't that much better than the Barbizon, but I did have a television set that Aaron had delivered to me.

One afternoon he called. I could hear in his voice that he had a cold. He told me he didn't have anyone to take care of him. He also said he wanted us to get married. Aaron was always a big baby when he got sick, so I wasn't buying what he was selling.

An hour later Aaron called again. This time he told me he had just spoken with my parents and had gotten their blessing for us to get married. It didn't matter that I had just signed a lease or that I would somehow have to get the television set back to California. I packed everything up and flew home to California. Six weeks later, Aaron and I were married on November 23, 1968. We had an intimate ceremony in front of immediate family at the apartment home of my parents at Sierra Towers.

After the ceremony, we all went down to the party room and had a surprise reception with eighty of our close friends and family. Nobody knew we had gotten married until they arrived. Our first dance as husband and wife was to "My Funny Valentine," which we had danced to the night we met at the Daisy.

Aaron always liked the way I looked best when I didn't have any makeup on and my hair was pulled back into a ponytail. It was always so telling to me. Even though he had been such a playboy and had to overcome his fears about giving marriage a second try, once we were married, I knew it would be forever.

6

Mrs. Spelling, I Presume

Aaron had to be on set in Bronson Canyon on Monday morning, so we didn't take a honeymoon. My husband also happened to be the inventor of the "staycation," so he arranged for us to spend a luxurious weekend at the Bel-Air hotel. His show *The Mod Squad*, which had started airing on ABC a couple of months before our wedding, was already getting a lot of attention. The program was more than just "groovy," it really was socially conscious and reflected what was going on in our country at the time. The antiwar movement, women's rights, racial issues, and child neglect were just a few of the topics the show explored.

The Mod Squad was actually the first show ever to depict an African American character as equal to a Caucasian character. ABC was very concerned about one episode where Linc gave Julie a friendly kiss on the cheek. They were up in arms about it at the edit and wanted to cut it out, but Aaron didn't see anything wrong with it and refused. This new twist on the American crime drama was popular with the youth market as well as adults. It was the first of so many of Aaron's shows that the whole family could watch together, and it was his breakthrough hit.

In addition to *The Mod Squad*, Aaron was very busy shooting what seemed like one television movie of the week after another. If I wanted to see my husband, I had to go out to set to visit him. One time I took my brand-new Corvette out to location in Lancaster. I parked too close to the set, and a big sound boom rigged above the set fell onto the fiberglass hood of the car and left a massive crater-size hole. I tried to be mature about it—after all, nobody was hurt—but I was pretty devastated about the damage to my beautiful car.

Not long after we were married, Aaron had an important meeting with the president of ABC. They scheduled a drinks meeting at the Beverly Hills Hotel. Aaron was very nervous and asked me to come along for moral support. Naturally I agreed. The only thing was that Aaron didn't want the president to see that he had brought "the missus" along. So instead of valet parking and letting me go off to entertain myself somewhere on the hotel property while he had his meeting, Aaron left me parked just outside the hotel on a side street. We thought he'd only be an hour, but it turned out to be two hours. Mind you, this was before cell phones and iPads, so it was a long two hours sitting in the car. In all honesty, I didn't mind. I was nervous and excited for him. When he finally returned to the car, he was ecstatic because ABC had just offered him the deal that would allow him to create Aaron Spelling Productions.

It was incredible to see all of this happening for Aaron. He was so brilliant and had worked so hard to get here. Still, I was starting to have identity issues. I loved being Mrs. Spelling, but I wanted to hang on to Candy, too. I think these feelings are common for all young wives, but most of my friends from high school had married and moved away, so I had nobody to share this with. My mother had cagey advice for me about always charging household expenses so they wouldn't be deducted from my allowance, but what I was experiencing was definitely not something she would have understood.

Part of my responsibility as Mrs. Spelling was to socialize with the wives of Aaron's collaborators and the network executives he did business with on a daily basis. They were a nice group of women, but they were twenty years older than I was. We didn't have anything in common. We couldn't even talk about our children because I didn't have any yet. Honestly, I also found them very intimidating.

Edie Wasserman was the "better half" of Lew Wasserman, the most powerful man in Hollywood. Edie herself was a woman of conviction who was very involved with different causes and a great champion of the Motion Picture and Television Fund. The organization offers social programs and financial assistance to professionals in the motion picture and television industries.

Doris Stein was the wife of visionary ophthalmologist Jules Stein, who founded the Jules Stein Eye Institute. Doris was a woman of purpose who was the inspiration for the creation of the institute. She devoted herself to initiatives to combat blindness around the globe.

Janet de Cordova was the wife of Johnny Carson's longtime executive producer, Freddie de Cordova. Their home in the Trousdale section of Beverly Hills was the center of the Hollywood society. Janet herself was known as the "Duchess of Trousdale."

The lunches had these awkward moments that I just dreaded. The ladies always liked a glass or two of chilled white wine with their lunch. They didn't worry that it wasn't five o'clock yet. I tried this once with hazardous results. I was drowsy for the rest of the day. I was already having trouble getting out of bed in the morning because I was mildly depressed, and I didn't need to spend my afternoon in a haze.

Aaron was from the same generation as my mother. He didn't talk about these kinds of things. When I tried hinting at my discomfort by mentioning the drinking, his answer was simple: "Well, just don't drink, then."

He was so secure he didn't even want anything monogrammed. I still remember him saying, "I know who I am and I know these are my shirts." That was how I wanted to feel. It suddenly occurred to me that all of my credit cards were in the name of Mrs. Aaron Spelling. Even though I had come into the marriage with my own money, more money, in fact, than my husband, nothing said Candy Spelling.

I'll never forget going to Robinson's department store in Beverly Hills one afternoon. The store was built in a midcentury modern style of architecture and was adjacent to the Beverly Hilton hotel on Wilshire Boulevard. I had my eye on a Judith Leiber purse, and I had been visiting it for several months. Aaron had just started making enough money that I felt I could indulge myself and buy the purse. When I got to Robinson's, the purse was on sale, so I thought, "Okay, I'm buying this purse!" When it came time to pay, I pulled out one of Aaron's credit cards that he had given me. I guess he hadn't changed the name on the card yet, so it said, "Mr. Aaron Spelling." Not even Mrs. Aaron Spelling.

I was wearing a pair of blue jeans and had no makeup on, so I probably looked much younger than I was at the time. The saleswoman asked me for my driver's license, but instead of that resolving the issue, I felt like I had set off a silent alarm. Suddenly salespeople were running around locking things down, frantically dialing the phone, and then I was escorted upstairs to the credit office. I stood there with my face flushing scarlet as they tried to reach Aaron to confirm I was his wife. The sale was approved, but I was truly humiliated.

On the way out of the store, I saw a sweater that I liked on a shelf. I asked the saleswoman how much it was and she said, "Oh, it's much more money than you can afford." I tried the sweater on hoping it would look wonderful on me so I could buy it. Unfortunately, it did not look great on me, so I left without it. I remember wishing I had bought it just to prove a point, but I think part of me knew even then that it was an issue of self-worth and not the sweater.

I was hardly a bird in a gilded cage, but I had definitely married a very traditional man with incredible ambition and drive. I was trying to find balance and not lose myself in his identity. Fortunately, it was not long after that we decided to remodel our first house on Palm Drive. Managing the remodel played to my strengths. I was good with money and decisive, and my double Virgo astrological sign made me perfect for overseeing all the details of the construction. It was a good reminder of qualities I had always been proud of and appreciated about myself.

7

Hollywood-Style Affection

I had come a long way from the shy girl who locked herself in the bathroom at Rock Hudson's house when I was first dating Aaron. Still, I don't think anything could have prepared me for socializing with the famous faces that Aaron was friendly with on daily basis. It's funny because my godfather, Howard Koch, was an Academy Award–winning screenwriter and a playwright who had worked with Orson Welles, Humphrey Bogart, and Joan Fontaine. Growing up, my parents frequented the Mocambo, a nightclub on the Sunset Strip, and they were friendly with Harry Ritz of the Ritz Brothers. The Ritz Brothers were the archrivals of the Marx Brothers, and Sid Caesar had called Harry "the funniest man alive." Later as a teenager, I had my own experiences with celebrities at Jax and of course the Daisy.

Aaron's world was different. He had an intimacy with these icons of the silver screen. It wasn't Aaron taking advantage of a photo op with Johnny Mathis or Van Cliburn at a big Hollywood party. He had a closeness with legendary actors that only a writer who truly understood them and had created parts for them could have. Aaron had deep roots in Hollywood going back to his first-ever script he sold to Jane Wyman in 1954. By coincidence, the last publicity still taken of Ronald Reagan as an actor was a shot of him in full cowboy costume from Aaron's show *Burke's Law.*

My first glimpse into this other world came on a trip we took to New York together shortly after we were married. It was selling season, so Aaron had business in New York. Among other things, he was going to show a pilot. We took a two-and-a-half-day train trip across the country. Aaron reserved two rooms, and they removed the wall between them so we could have lower berths and private bathrooms. The dining car was fabulous, and the trip really was very charming and romantic in its own way. I remember it being a lot of fun.

In Joliet, Illinois, a reporter got on board to interview Aaron. He traveled with us the rest of the way to Penn Station in New York. Marlo Thomas, the eldest child of Aaron's former producing partner Danny Thomas, arranged for us to stay at The Plaza Hotel in a beautiful suite overlooking Central Park. Aaron had known Marlo almost her entire life because he and Danny had been producing partners for so long. Needless to say, our suite was a far cry from my quarters at the Barbizon Hotel.

There on the table waiting for us was a stunning bouquet of flowers with a darling little watering can. The note card had a warm welcome message along with instructions for watering the flowers. The card was signed by none other than Joan Crawford. Joan was one of Aaron's oldest and dearest friends. They had known each other for ages and had worked together. In 1959, he had written an episode called "Rebel Ranger" for her in *Zane Grey Theatre. Zane Grey Theatre* was a series based on the short stories of western author Zane Grey. Aaron had produced and written about twenty of them. Joan played a Confederate widow, Stella Faring, who tries to reclaim her former home and her son's birthplace from its Unionist owner.

That night we made our way to the Upper East Side to meet Joan. She had an enormous apartment where everything inside was coated with thick, clear plastic to keep it clean. I remember being taken aback and thinking, "And here I thought I was a neat freak." Right there in the living room, she had two adorable puppies in a playpen.

Joan was a formidable woman. She was tall and big boned. Not overweight, just a larger-framed woman. I sat down to play with the puppies. Meanwhile, Joan invited Aaron to her bedroom to watch her get dressed. I know it sounds strange but I wasn't worried at all—it was nothing. Aaron and Joan had never been romantic, and he had already warned me that this was something Joan did with her male friends. Because she was Joan Crawford, she knew there would be no protests from either one of us. So while Aaron paid his respects to Joan by watching her dress herself, I kept myself entertained with the puppies. I always felt like I got the better end of the bargain on that one.

I soon learned she had other quirks. For one thing, Joan always drank 100-proof vodka. In fact, at the restaurant where we had dinner that evening with Generoso Pope Jr., the owner of the *National Enquirer,* the waiter brought her special bottle of vodka to the semiprivate room where we were dining. The vodka had been stored there for her, chilled to perfection, and then poured for her.

We were having a lovely dinner until Joan decided to order blueberry yogurt for dessert. Yogurt happens to be a food I don't care for at all. It's one of those foods that I don't even like to look at. It was worse back then since the yogurt wasn't creamy the way it is now. It was gloppy and full of curds. The waiter brought a bowl of the blueberry yogurt out to the round table where we were sitting. Joan looked at me.

"Candy, you must taste this! It's absolutely delicious."

I politely declined, but Joan Crawford was not accepting a "no" from Aaron Spelling's young wife. She dug deep into the bowl with a large tablespoon and then brought it to my lips. The yogurt spilled over the spoon. The last thing I wanted to do was insult my husband's friend, but I was worried I would gag on the yogurt. Joan practically forced the spoon past my lips. I was so grateful I was able to swallow the yogurt without it coming back up. It was disgusting, but of course I said it was delicious. (Years later I would tell this story to Tori's godmother, Barbara Stanwyck, and she shared that Joan had once force-fed her an entire piece of calf's liver.)

Just before the trip, Aaron had bought me a beautiful and unique ring. It was actually three rings in one that interlocked, and each ring was a flower. It was one emerald, one ruby, and one sapphire. Together they looked like one ring. I absolutely loved them. They were very sweet, and Aaron was very proud of his purchase. I wore them out with Joan that night. Aaron happened to ask her if she had noticed the ring. Joan looked at Aaron as if she were in her most regal role ever and spoke with grand politesse.

"Darling. Until you can afford to buy your wife jewelry that is important, I would simply advise that you just buy her candy and flowers."

Aaron never bought me anything small or cutesy again. After that night I think his perspective shifted, and he came to believe that the jewelry he bought for me was a measure of his success and not just a token of his affection. I never asked him for any of the jewelry he gave me, but every time he bought me an incredible piece, I thought of Joan Crawford.

Frenemies

It was actually my jewelry collection that ignited Elizabeth Taylor's unofficial rivalry with me. Aaron compulsively bought me jewelry and Elizabeth obsessively collected it, so I suppose it was inevitable. Aaron had known Elizabeth for years, and like everyone else, she adored him. They had worked together and were also part of the same social circles. When Aaron divorced Carolyn and needed to find a place to live, he had rented Elizabeth's old house. There were avocado trees in the back, and his dog Adam used to eat the ones that fell from the trees.

The first time I met Elizabeth was in the mid-1980s at a party given by "Mr. and Mrs. Hollywood," Lew Wasserman and his wife, Edie. For thirty years, Lew Wasserman had been the top guy in Tinseltown. He and his wife Edie had been married for about fifty years at this point. She was very much his partner as well as an incredible philanthropist. They were known for their lavish, over-the-top parties that brought out all the Hollywood stars as well as the powerful politicos. This evening was no different. It was one of those dazzling nights where they had transformed a soundstage at Universal Studios and filled it with famous faces.

I don't recall what dress I was wearing, but I distinctly remember that I was wearing an emerald suite that Aaron had given me. Elizabeth was—as was her style—more than fashionably late. The crowds parted as she made a royal entrance befitting the Queen of the Nile. She must have been in her early fifties, but she was still magnificently beautiful. Her eyes were absolutely captivating, as were the jewels that adorned her.

"Aaron! Darling!"

There I was on Aaron's arm, and she acted like I was invisible. She was very touchy-feely with my husband and cool as cucumber with me. As luck would have it, Elizabeth was wearing the legendary Bulgari emerald suite given to her by Richard Burton after they finished filming *Cleopatra*. I remember the media sensation that surrounded his gift to her at the time. Burton had half-jokingly said that the only word Elizabeth knew in Italian was Bulgari.

Two women at the same gala wearing emeralds is no different than two women wearing the same designer dress on a red carpet. When Aaron introduced me to Elizabeth, I felt her violet eyes lock onto my emeralds and make a quick assessment. It was unusual to see women with suites of jewelry like ours, and I could see she felt competitive with me. I never would have admitted this to Aaron, but my Van Cleef & Arpels emeralds were outdone by her Bulgari emeralds.

Elizabeth had been a superstar since she was a young girl, so it wasn't surprising that she needed to command all the attention. Over the years we would socialize with Elizabeth, so I did get to know her better. I wouldn't say we were friends, but we were friends with many of the same people. Having been shy myself, I recognized that Elizabeth was actually shy too. Instead of retreating into herself like I did for so many years, Elizabeth put on this aloof and dramatic personality to keep everyone at a safe and humble distance. I do think this was the bond she shared with Michael Jackson, who, like her, had also become a sensation at a very young age.

Sometime near 2000, Michael and Elizabeth went to a jewelry auction together, and he bought her the now-famous "Monkey Necklace" that originally belonged to Baroness Sandra di Portanova. The necklace was designed for the baroness by her husband Ricky di Portanova. Its principal design was interlocking monkeys encrusted with pavé diamonds, rubies, and emeralds. Truthfully, the whimsical necklace was a far cry from the sophisticated designs Elizabeth was accustomed to, but Michael had given it to her with so much love that she wore it with pride. I remember seeing the two of them at The Carousel Ball shortly after he had presented it to her. They were like two kids on Christmas showing off their new toy.

The great irony of the "Monkey Necklace" is that what gave it real value was its history with Michael Jackson and Elizabeth Taylor. When it was first auctioned after the death of the baroness in 2000, it sold for a relatively modest $55,000 and included a set of matching earrings. Michael paid an undisclosed amount for just the necklace. Eleven years later when Christie's auctioned off Elizabeth Taylor's jewelry collection for charity, the necklace garnered an impressive $260,000 and became a piece of Hollywood history.

9

Life Imitating Art

It wasn't all rivalry, diva tantrums, and tabloid fodder off camera. Many of these movie stars had come through the ranks of the Hollywood studio system together and had tremendous sensitivity and respect for one another. In many ways they really were one big Hollywood family.

I think the first time I made this observation was at a birthday party for Elizabeth. She was turning fifty-five that year, so Academy and Grammy Award–winning composers Burt Bacharach and his then-wife Carole Bayer Sager, who is also a Grammy and Academy Award–winning songwriter, hosted the party at their home in Bel-Air. It was a casual type of party, so I wasn't wearing what Joan Crawford would have called "important jewelry," and neither was the birthday girl. Unless it was a gala or a ball, it really wasn't appropriate.

As always, Elizabeth was fashionably late so that she could make her grand entrance. When we arrived at the party, there in the middle of the living room holding court was the legend of all female Hollywood legends—Miss Bette Davis. While she may have looked like a queen on her throne granting an audience to those who bowed before her, the truth was that Bette wasn't well at the time, so she couldn't get up out of the chair.

In 1965, Bette starred in a pilot for a TV sitcom that Aaron had written and produced. Even though she had won two Academy Awards, Bette was not above appearing on television. The show was called *The Decorator*. Bette played a cantankerous interior decorator who moves in with her clients so she can learn about their lifestyle and then decorate their homes. The show, which co-starred the scene-stealing Mary Wickes and Ed Begley, didn't get picked up by a network, so it never aired. I know how devastated Aaron was. In his book *Dark Victory: The Life of Bette Davis,* author Ed Sikov wrote, "She was very disappointed *The Decorator* didn't go. No, not disappointed—*hurt*. Very hurt."

The failure of *The Decorator* to get picked up obviously didn't hurt Bette's or Aaron's careers. All these years later, Aaron and Bette were still connected to one another. When Bette saw Aaron walk into the room, she rose up out of the chair and came over to embrace him. This made more than a few heads turn, including Michael Jackson, who was there that night with his bodyguard. Michael had been wanting to work with Aaron, but that night he had his eye set on making the acquaintance of Bette. Here he was, the biggest pop star in the world; he could have gone straight over to Bette and introduced himself. Instead he was so modest and such a gentleman that he waited for a proper introduction to her.

Aaron was doing his series *Hotel* at the time, and he had written parts for Bette and Elizabeth. Bette was originally going to play aristocrat Victoria Cabot, who ran the St. Gregory Hotel in the city of San Francisco where the show was set. He was very excited for the opportunity to work with both of them again. True to form, in Elizabeth's contract Aaron was required to buy her character strands of diamonds-by-the-yard and in the proviso Elizabeth would get to keep them. Aaron never said a word. He knew Elizabeth's standards and wanted to keep her happy. Unfortunately, Bette wasn't well and had to drop out of the show, so Aaron got the idea to replace her with Anne Baxter. It was life imitating art because Anne had played the ingénue in *All About Eve*. In the 1950 film directed by Joseph L. Mankiewicz, Anne's character maneuvers her way into the theater company and social circle of an aging stage actress played by Bette Davis. Before Anne would agree to take on the role in *Hotel*, she told Aaron that out of respect for Bette, she wanted to ask for her permission and her blessing first.

That evening led to Aaron and me getting to know Michael Jackson and his children, Paris and Prince, who were just little ones at the time. Aaron was working on a script for Michael. It was an idea based on the premise of the Pied Piper. Marvin Davis, who owned 20th Century Fox Studios, and George Lucas were also involved in the project. Like so many viable ideas, the project was shelved, but we did get to spend a lot of time with Michael.

Michael was the kindest person. He was so gentle and such a wonderful father. We were all guests at a small dinner party at the Davises' one night. Marvin's wife, Barbara, had bought Prince and Paris little electric cars, and they were zipping around the entryway of the house. There were bowls of candy around and the children wanted some. I still remember Michael crouching down and in a whisper of a voice telling them they couldn't have any candy until after dinner. It was magical the way his children listened to him. I felt like any other children at this age would have thrown a tantrum, but in this case, once again it was life imitating art. Paris and Prince understood, fell in line with their father's wishes, and patiently waited to have candy after their dinner.

10

Ain't That a Kick in the Head

Socializing was as much a part of Aaron's job as the writing was, and he loved every minute of it. I have this expression about people who can have an interesting conversation with anyone. I like to say, "He could talk to a bush." Aaron was without question one of these people. We didn't always go to star-studded parties or industry events. Sometimes we had cozy, low-key dinners with other couples. We also went to poker night at the home of Janet Leigh and her husband Bob Brandt. Janet was a sweet, down-to-earth woman. When I first met her, I couldn't get the image from *Psycho* of her being stabbed to death so violently in the shower out of my mind.

We were also invited to the home of actress Natalie Wood for dinner on more than one occasion. She was already divorced from Robert Wagner and was married to British producer Richard Gregson. She was a new mother and had stepped back from her career so she could raise her baby. Natalie had this innocence about her, and those amazing eyes of hers were even more incredible in person. She was taking her role as a stay-at-home mom very seriously. She was spending a lot of time in the kitchen and really did cook from the heart. Unfortunately, cooking was not her strongest suit, and I remember Aaron and me joking about what Natalie's "mystery meat would be this time."

What fascinated me most about Natalie was that here she was, this glamorous, sexy, and iconic beauty. One of the biggest movie stars of all time. I mean *West Side Story*, *Rebel Without a Cause,* and who could forget her with Warren Beatty in Elia Kazan's *Splendor in the Grass*? Despite all of this, she was as self-conscious as the rest of us women are, if not more. She always wore this big, chunky bracelet on her wrist to cover a bump she had on the joint from when she had broken it. It always amazed me that these stunningly beautiful women could have any insecurity at all.

Another couple we had fun with were Dick and Dolly Martin. Dick was the co-host of the comedy sketch show *Rowan & Martin's Laugh-In*. The show was so funny and so different for the time. After the show ended, Dick developed a career as a television director. At the time, he was directing episodes of *The Bob Newhart Show*. He would go on to become a sought-after director who worked on at least a dozen television series. Dick's wife was a gorgeous Playboy Playmate appropriately named Dolly. Dolly had also been in Russ Meyer's campy film *Beyond the Valley of the Dolls*. Dick and Dolly used to host movie night at their in-home theater. This was a big deal in those days since not everybody had home theaters.

It was at Dick and Dolly's house that I first met Dean Martin and his new wife, Cathy. She was Dean's third wife, and I just loved both of them from the moment I met them. It sounds funny to say, but since being married to Aaron, Dean and Cathy were the first friends I had made on my own. And Dean was the first celebrity I had befriended before Aaron did.

In 1974, the six of us plus Bob Newhart and his wife Ginny took a trip to Las Vegas to see Frank Sinatra's comeback performance at Caesar's Palace. Even under serious peer pressure, Aaron refused to fly in the private jet that Dean had chartered. In fact, when he first heard about the trip and the private plane, he said, "Well, that's it. We're not going." I was really upset and started to cry, which made Aaron reconsider. So while everyone else in our party traveled on the jet, we drove.

The MGM Grand had just opened in 1973, and it was the first super luxury resort on the Las Vegas Strip. It had just over two thousand rooms and this decadent fountain that was lit up at night. The hotel was incredible, and, at the time, it was the place to stay in Sin City. When we all met up in the lobby of the brand-new MGM hotel, Dean said that they had waved to us as their plane flew over our car chugging along the desert road. At the registration desk, Dean requested a room lower than the fourth floor. It turned out he had a phobia of elevators. Sure enough, when Aaron heard that, he said he didn't want a room above the fourth floor either. It didn't happen often, but this was one of those times where I put my foot down.

"Aaron, that's Dean's phobia, not yours! We can stay on a higher floor. You already have your own phobia." I just couldn't imagine if in addition to flying, Aaron also stopped taking elevators.

The show at Caesar's was really something else that night. Trying to get through the throngs of manic people to our VIP seats was a little frightening. Even with private security guards and Las Vegas police cordoning off the VIP area, fans of Dean were reaching, clawing, and doing anything they could to get his attention or talk to him. I thought I had seen it all at Hollywood premieres or nights out with Aaron where people, one after another, approached him. This was something else altogether. It was that evening that I realized the magnitude of the power these stars have over their fans.

After Frank's show we all headed for the casino to our own private blackjack table. Ironically, none of us were really gamblers. Dean jumped behind the table and assumed the role of dealer. Aaron and Dick partnered up but refused to play with their own money. It was funny to watch all these men who were creative geniuses and risk takers play cards. They were so hesitant and completely overthought everything.

Dean, on the other hand, just went for it. He went bust every time. Cathy and I could see his cards and couldn't understand why he hit when he already had twenty-one. We were finally able to persuade Aaron and Dick to take the plunge and gamble with their own money. Dick had been a bartender and referred to martinis as "see-throughs," so I kept joking that he'd had a few too many "see-throughs." Meanwhile, Dick was playing a big hand and all the while he kept saying that he didn't gamble. He kept on that he was afraid he was going to lose all his money and have to go back to being a bartender. No such luck! Dick and Aaron ended up winning and winning big, but Dick was so drunk that Aaron and I had to escort him and all his chips to his room.

In the morning, Dick came knocking on our door. He wanted to know where the pile of chips in his room had come from. We told him that he had won them playing blackjack.

"You know I don't gamble, Candy. Now really, tell me where all these chips came from." Aaron couldn't stop laughing, so Dick probably thought we were playing a joke on him. The conversation we were having was not unlike the sketches on *Laugh-In* when Dick always played the frustrated straight man. He remained adamant. It just wasn't possible. He simply didn't gamble.

I explained one last time that he had been so drunk that Aaron and I had literally tucked him into bed. Dick was absolutely mortified. He obviously had had a few too many "see-throughs."

11

The King of Cool

Of all the friendships we developed over the years, our friendship with Dean Martin stands out as one of the most special. We met one night at one of Dick and Dolly's movie nights. Sometimes the movies we watched were comedies, which I sometimes dreaded because of this problem I have when I laugh. I hate to admit it, but when I really get going, I mean a real belly laugh, I sound like a seal. Well, at one of those movie nights, we were watching something that was very funny, and it happened. My inner seal came out, and I was exposed in front of "The King of Cool." Dean couldn't believe what he was hearing. He literally looked away from the movie over at me, and now he was laughing his heart out too. It wasn't mean-spirited, it was more like a big brother making fun of his sister. Aaron got a big kick out of the whole thing and somehow, after that brief albeit ridiculous moment, we were all bonded.

One of the biggest misconceptions about Dean was that he was an alcoholic who stumbled around all day. In his 1996 obituary, *People* magazine printed the headline, "Dean Martin perfected a 100-Proof Wink." They added that Dean's "image slowly evaporated like uncorked Scotch." This just goes to show how little the media sometimes knows and how there usually is more to the story. As far as I could tell, the problem Dean had was that every night he would take one of his prescription sleeping pills, even if he'd had a few drinks. This, as you can imagine, did not produce good results. I saw this firsthand when Dean and Cathy would come out to stay with us at our beach house in Malibu.

Dean was so much fun to have around. He had this adolescent sense of mischief about him that brought so much energy into the house. In the mornings, we would wake up to Dean driving a bucket of brand-new golf balls into the Pacific Ocean. Watching him out there hitting one ball after another out into the water made me realize that Dean really was a loner. When he chose to be with people, he was very present, not to mention big on teasing. For the longest time he couldn't remember the name of Aaron's Belgian shepherd, Adam. Dean always called him Bruno, probably because Adam was a very large, dark creature. I would always correct Dean, "It's Adam!"

One morning Aaron and I woke up and Dean was still groggy from his sleeping-pill cocktail from the night before. He apologized for stepping on Bruno. I had no idea what he was talking about, and then I remembered that Adam liked to sleep on the landing of the staircase that led to the second floor of the house.

"It's Adam!" I yelled.

I looked over at Dean, and he had that sly, quiet smile of his on his face. He was just teasing me. He really had stepped on Adam, but fortunately Adam was large enough to handle it. At worst, Adam had probably just been startled by Dean. That particular morning Dean also apologized for eating all the cookies on the counter. Once again, I was baffled. Suddenly I realized Dean was referring to the freshly baked cinnamon rolls I had left out for us to have in the morning. They weren't cookies, and Dean had eaten all four of them.

Sadly, Dean and Cathy divorced a couple of years later. We didn't see much of him after that. I think he must have felt like ours had been a couples thing and he wasn't part of a couple anymore, so he was off on his own.

It was almost a decade later that I drove out to the set of *Hotel* to visit Aaron. It was pouring rain, and they were shooting way out at Zuma Beach in Malibu. Wonderful actor Richard Kiley, who had worked with Aaron on *The Mod Squad,* was guest-starring in this episode of *Hotel*. Richard was also a stage actor and had won two Tony Awards, so I always found him interesting to talk to. He said something so poignant that afternoon as we sat there in the rain. He said that he wanted to hide behind the character he was playing at the time. This immediately made me think of Dean. I had seen him hide behind the drunken character he had created. He put on his "drunk act" for fans and for people he didn't want to interact with. It was his defense mechanism that nobody would have ever thought to look beyond.

A couple of years later, Dean's oldest son, Dean Paul Martin, was killed in a plane crash. Ironically his plane crashed in the same area where a private charter carrying Frank Sinatra's mother had crashed ten years earlier. I don't think Dean was ever able to recover from this loss. We heard from friends that ran into him that he had become a recluse. On occasion other friends saw him alone at restaurants he had always frequented, looking like a ghost of himself.

I will always remember Dean as the kind, talented, and generous person that he was. He was always taking care of everybody else. Aaron had to get used to the fact that Dean was always quick to reach for the check. He was quicker than even Aaron was, which was really something.

I used to say that Dean was truly a Mensch. In Yiddish this means he was a person of goodness and integrity. He wasn't Jewish, but I liked describing him that way anyway. And because he wasn't Jewish, in some way it was even more of an honor.

12

The Mother Is Born

I always wanted children. Not just because that's what women from my generation did without even giving it a second thought, but because I really wanted to be a mother. Like most career-driven men, Aaron didn't have children on the forefront of his mind. He was busy writing, shooting pilots, and selling shows. Children weren't planned as meticulously as they are these days. I think we all just assumed it would happen naturally.

After our "Staycation Honeymoon" at the Bel-Air hotel, it seemed like every time somebody congratulated us, it was followed by the question, "When are you having a baby?" I was still writing out thank-you cards for wedding gifts and getting settled into our home and into our new life together. As time went on, I wouldn't exactly say I had baby fever, but I was definitely taken aback by the question and felt the pressure.

Forty-one years ago there weren't fertility specialists. I was only twenty-three years old and was counting on Mother Nature to do her part—but she didn't. As time marched on, years even, I was so frustrated and felt badly about myself. Aaron wasn't keen on adopting, but it seemed like our only viable option. He loved me and knew what having children meant to me. He made it clear that he was willing to adopt, even though the process wasn't an easy one.

We visited an adoption agency and subjected ourselves to all the rigors of the process. The next step was simple—you wait. We waited for what seemed like an eternity, and then finally our names had moved to the top of the list— and wouldn't you know it, I found out I was pregnant! We were terribly excited.

I was fortunate to have had a healthy pregnancy. I had cravings for salty foods like pickles and caviar, of all things. I also made more than a few trips to my high-school haunt, Dolores's, for burgers and fries. A month before my due date, on May 16, 1973, I gave birth to a baby girl weighing in at 5 pounds, 2 ounces. It was a very special day. She was such a beauty.

Aaron and I had already chosen her name: Victoria Davey Spelling. I'd had names floating around in my head for years. I gave it a lot of thought because when I was growing up, I knew kids with unfortunate names like Pepper Salters and Ginger Snap. I felt so badly for those kids. I don't think anyone, least of all the kids, were charmed by those kitschy names. I knew if I had a girl, I wanted to name her Victoria. I always loved the name. It was so feminine, elegant, and regal. The middle name Davey came from Aaron's father. I knew Victoria would be too long and too formal for people to use. It seemed inevitable that my daughter's friends and teachers would call her by the nickname "Vicki," which I really wanted to avoid.

Barbara Stanwyck was a very close and dear friend of ours, so we asked her to be the baby's godmother. She bought us this gorgeous, giant pram that we used for both of our children and lent to friends over the years. It was actually Barbara who suggested that we take control of the nickname situation by calling our baby girl "Tori" right from the start. It was such a brilliant idea. There was no way to abbreviate Tori, and this name ended up really suiting her. So really it's Barbara whom Tori has to thank for all the different ways she's been able to brand herself over the years: InvenTORI, EdiTORIial, sTORI telling, and CelebraTORI.

Apparently my body was on a five-year cycle because in 1978, our son Randall Gene Spelling was born. Aaron and I both really liked the nickname

Randy, so it was easy for us to pick the name this time. We gave him the middle name Gene after my mother and my grandfather. Randy was born on October 9, more than two months ahead of his due date. We were so thrilled again and felt so blessed. Because he was born at six and half months, he was this tiny little baby weighing just over two pounds. It was two and a half months before we could bring him home from the hospital.

Motherhood was daunting but I happily settled into it. It was fascinating to see how fatherhood changed Aaron. When both kids were born, it was very difficult for him because they were such fragile and helpless creatures. Fatherhood also made Aaron more sentimental. He loved those babies more than he ever could have imagined. As they grew up, his favorite thing was to be with them and do anything that would bring smiles to their faces.

I always had a good sense of humor, and once I became a mother, I fully embraced it. I think it was also about this time that I became a fan of American humorist Erma Bombeck and her musings on the dangers of raising children and training husbands. In her May 12, 1974 *Dayton Journal Herald* column, "When God Created Mothers," Bombeck wrote, "When the good Lord was creating mothers, he was into his sixth day of 'overtime' when the angel appeared and said. 'You're doing a lot of fiddling around on this one.'

"The Lord said, 'Have you read the specs on this order? She has to be completely washable, but not plastic; Have 180 moveable parts . . . all replaceable; Run on black coffee and leftovers; Have a lap that disappears when she stands up; A kiss that can cure anything from a broken leg to a disappointed love affair; And six pairs of hands.'"

Like any other woman who entered into motherhood, my life was forever changed when I became one. The day that I gave birth to Tori, I promised myself that I would be the perfect mother. I think especially because I had had such an unhappy childhood, I wanted my children to have perfect childhoods. I imagine that all mothers make this promise to themselves. We are convinced that we'll take all the good qualities that our own mothers passed down to us and use them in even better ways with our own children. Likewise, we promise to toss out all of the bad and do things for our children the way we wanted it done for ourselves when we were kids.

Aaron had been the skinniest member in a family of five children. When he was growing up, it fell on him to wait in the bread line for the day-old bread. Aaron's mother, Pearl, was incredibly loving and self-sacrificing. He had many memories of her going to bed hungry so her children could eat. She would pretend she wasn't hungry and turn in for the night. So for Aaron, giving to our children meant giving them every possible material object they might want. And every celebration, whether it was a birthday, holiday, or anniversary, was designed to be a magical experience that would bring joy to the whole family.

As for me, when I was a child I longed for a mother who would treat me like the child that I was and not like I was her pupil at a finishing school. When I was a little girl, I desperately wanted a dog, but my mother didn't care for animals. She used to say to me, "When you get married, you can have as many dogs as you want." Once I was a mother, I wanted my children to have the many things I didn't have as a child, not the least of which was affection and, of course, a dog or maybe even two.

Our children were definitely allowed to have pets. In fact, I felt like Farmer Gray from the 1950s Terry-Toons comics. At one point we had six dogs, a mixed pack of poodles and bichons. We also had birds, fish, turtles, frogs, and tadpoles. I found the tadpoles absolutely frightening. I had nightmares of the full-grown frogs taking over the house like one of the Ten Plagues of Egypt. I could see them hopping all over the kitchen, in the oven, inside the refrigerator, and up the stairs into our bedroom. Worst of all, I envisioned them hopping up onto our bed and all over me while I was sleeping.

At one point, we also had rabbits. I naively thought they would make cute Easter presents and great pets. I had no idea rabbits would be such hard work. The cages were hard to keep clean, not to mention deodorized. Our fluffy Easter rabbits started off as adorable little bunnies with those unbelievably cute pink ears. Before too long they had evolved into these mad March hares that fought at night. It was so awful, and I felt so badly for the sweet Angora rabbit who was always being attacked by the white New Zealand rabbit.

Even in separate cages, the rabbits seem to antagonize one another, so we'd wake up every morning to a big mess of hay, rabbit pee, and rabbit poop scattered all around the table where we kept the cages at night. I had been trying to enforce Tori and Randy's responsibility for cleaning up after their pets, but after about the fourth consecutive day, the kids were done. I knew that we needed to find another home for the rabbits, so I called the owner of the pet shop to see if I could enlist his help. I explained that I didn't want any money back, I just needed his assistance in rehoming the rabbits. The storeowner refused to help. He explained that Easter was over, and full-grown rabbits were not the popular commodity cute baby bunnies were.

Looking back, I'm sure I wasn't the first frantic mother calling with a plea for help. In fact, hysterical mothers were probably part of his retail season. I was desperate and needed a solution, so I did what any desperate mother would do. I loaded the bunnies in their cages into the backseat of my BMW and drove straight to the pet shop. When there was no one around, I unloaded the cages and left them at the shop's front door. I felt like none other than Lucy Ricardo as I sat in my car nervously waiting for someone to come out of the shop and take them in. Finally someone did. That was when I drove away. I called the owner later to confess and apologize. We had a good laugh, and he said he understood. He had been able to find them a new home, so I felt a lot less guilty.

If only the trials and the tribulations of the pet bunnies had been the hardest part of parenting, I would have been in pretty good shape. I honestly can't think of anything harder than raising a teenager, except of course raising two teenagers. Compared to adolescence, late-night feedings and the "terrible twos" seemed like a cakewalk. The hormonal teenage years are truly the acid test for all parents.

I've always said that Tori has "the eye of the tiger." This was true of her even as a little girl. She knew what she wanted and truly thrived on being Aaron's daughter. Tori had lots of friends, did well in school, and was accepted to the University of Southern California on her own merit. When she got serious about being an actress, she met with a talent manager who told her she needed to "be hungry." Tori took this advice to heart, raised the bar on herself, and I think has exceeded expectations.

My son, Randy, was a different kind of child. He was a sensitive and emotional kid who didn't like competitive environments. He may be more like his mom in that way. When we tried enrolling him at the prestigious Harvard School (brother school to Tori's all-girl school), he was very clear that he didn't want to go there. We got Randy a full-time tutor weeks before school was supposed to start and tried another school that wasn't the right fit either. Finally we found Montclair Prep in the San Fernando Valley, and it turned out to be the perfect school for Randy. It was a much more nurturing and collaborative environment and truthfully not something I would have thought to look for in a school; I'd gone straight for the academics.

Hindsight really is twenty-twenty. I see now that in my quest to be the perfect mother and create the picture-perfect life for my children, I was too focused on the bigger picture and not enough on the smaller brush strokes. The poet Maya Angelou really hit the nail on the head when she wrote, "I've learned that people will forget what you said, people will forget what you did, but people will never forget how you made them feel."

I feel badly that my children felt I wasn't affectionate enough. I thought I was. Having come from a family where there was no affection, my barometer was obviously off. I thought I was being nurturing by hiring a tutor for Randy and being open to different schools for him. I know now that he needed a different kind of nurturing.

Aaron and I definitely made mistakes, and if I had to do it all over again, I would change certain dynamics. First, and I think this goes on in a lot of households, I would not have allowed Aaron to be the "good cop." I was always the "bad cop" and even when I wasn't, Aaron hung the rap on me. I would definitely go back and institute a united front for the benefit of the children and the family as a whole.

With time, I see now that it would have been beneficial for the children to have had responsibilities around the house. It would have been a battle with my overindulgent husband, but we really should have taught the kids to do more for themselves. They should have earned the electronic gadgets, the designer clothes, and the fancy cars.

Both of my children are parents now with their own children. I think they are learning the complexities of being "Mommy" and "Daddy" and how as a parent you are graded on a curve. I don't think Tori ever forgave me for returning the rabbits to the pet shop. A few years ago, she and her husband got rabbits for their own kids. Instead of fighting, her rabbits multiplied the way those rabbits are known to do.

I guess the good news for them is that these days, there are bunny rescues who can help rehome those rascally rabbits if the situation gets out of control.

13

Family Matters

Aaron's father, David, died just before we met, but I had a wonderful relationship with Aaron's mother, Pearl. When I met her, she was living on her own in Texas and used to come visit Aaron in Los Angeles with her sister Lena. The three of them were very close, so Pearl and Lena would come stay in his little two-bedroom house.

In Texas terms, the sisters were a "real hoot." One morning I stopped by to visit with them. Pearl was at the kitchen counter making tea. I asked her how she had slept. "Lena kept me up with her snoring." Then I went into the living room where Lena was sitting and I asked her how she'd slept. "Pearl kept me up all night with her snoring."

What was so amazing about these women was that they had grown up poor and raised their children during the Depression, yet at their core, they were happy individuals. Sadly, Pearl died just before Aaron and I were married.

My mother was born Augusta Gene. When she was older, she legally changed her first name to Gene, from her father's name Eugene. My mother was Hungarian by descent. Her mother Helen was Hungarian by birth and married a Hungarian immigrant, Eugene Rosen, here in the United States. My grandfather Eugene owned all the meat concessions in Grand Central Market and was able to create a very comfortable lifestyle for my grandmother Helen, my mother, and her brother, Milton.

My grandparents eventually settled in Beverly Hills, and that is where my mother went to high school. Eugene was president of Sinai Temple, where I am still a member today. I always loved when my mother told me about the horses and buggies that rode along Sunset Boulevard.

My mother's brother, Milton, went into the meat concession business with my grandfather Eugene and ended up stealing most of the business from his own father. This obviously led to a serious fracture in our family, and Milton ended up legally changing his last name to Melton so he wouldn't be a Rosen anymore. So somewhere out there I have cousins on the Rosen side who have the last name Melton.

Eugene and Helen fell on hard financial times after the situation with Milton. In those days a bride had a trousseau, which was a hope chest filled with the personal possessions of the bride. This included, among other things, the wedding dress, linens, household wares, and sometimes a dowry. When my mother got engaged to my father, my grandmother Helen scrubbed floors to earn the money for my mother's trousseau.

My father was Merritt Marer. His parents were Arthur and Ada Marer. They were both Russian immigrants who lived in Chicago. Arthur was a sophisticated man-about-town living the American Dream. At the age of forty-nine, he died of a heart attack in the arms of another woman. It may very well have been at the Copacabana in New York City. Wherever it was, I always picture martinis flowing in a smoke-filled room full of gorgeous showgirls, sexy cigarette girls, and splashy night-club acts.

My parents were obviously married at the time of my paternal grandfather Arthur's scandalous passing. Helen felt terrible for Ada, who was not only suddenly a young widow but was also betrayed by her husband. Helen's heart went out to Ada, and she started inviting her over to the house and out every-where with her and Eugene. Well, Ada and Eugene got a little closer than expected. Let's just say too close. Eugene and Ada had an affair, and then Eugene left Helen and married the widowed Ada.

Helen was absolutely humiliated and devastated. She was only in her fifties but never remarried or even went on one date. I always wondered how she must have felt being betrayed by someone she had shown so much kindness and compassion. I don't have a clear memory of how this affected my parents although it couldn't have been easy since technically they were now stepsiblings.

There's that expression "walls have ears," and at the time those ears were mine. My parents never directly told me what was happening, but I overheard most of the details. I do remember it was difficult for my mother because Helen was calling all the time and asking, "How could he do this to me?" Other than this we never discussed the "situation," even though it was a major crisis in our family.

We used to have these awkward family visits where we went to see Eugene and Ada. It was obviously very uncomfortable, but in keeping with the times and the way my family was, everybody maintained an air of civility. I was always amazed at how everyone ignored the giant elephant in the room.

When I was about fourteen years old, I found a letter in my mother's jewelry drawer that alluded to an affair my father was having. My mother had obviously elected to bury her head in the sand and ignore her husband's indiscretion. Meanwhile, she kept up appearances with expensive things and refined manners.

So this was the pattern in my family. Starting with my Uncle Milton, the men committed transgressions and the women in my family bore the burden. I suppose this was the role of women of that generation. These women seemed to have no voice and sadly no option for taking care of themselves unless of course they wanted to scrub floors.

Given my family background, it's no surprise that just a few years later I married Howard. Even though most of my high-school girlfriends were going to college, I relegated myself to a different category. I had an eye disorder called convergence insufficiency that made reading difficult. It is a neuromuscular anomaly that makes it impossible for my eyes to focus when looking at an object up close or reading. These days it's diagnosed in school-age children. Unfortunately, I wasn't diagnosed until I was an adult, so my entire academic life I was just considered "slow." All through high school, I had to find creative ways to study, like memory games and word association.

After graduation, Howard was my escape from my repressed home environment. The great irony of course was that my life with Howard was as isolating as my life with my family was. Women could drive and vote, but somehow it seemed that we were still living in the previous century.

14

Strangers: The Story of a Mother and Daughter

When Aaron and I chose the Saturday after Thanksgiving for our wedding date, I didn't give much thought to the fact that in some years our anniversary would actually fall on Thanksgiving Day. It was our fourth wedding anniversary that fell on the holiday, so we planned a Thanksgiving Day wedding anniversary dinner at the Bel-Air hotel.

There we were all gathered around the beautiful Thanksgiving table with my parents, and Aaron presented me with my anniversary gift. Because I have a hard time being the center of attention, I really would have preferred to open it in private with my husband. Always the showman, Aaron insisted I open it in front of my parents, so I did. It was a stunning diamond pin from Van Cleef & Arpels.

I don't know why I was so surprised by my mother's reaction, but until that very moment, I guess I was still naive. Instead of commenting on the thoughtfulness of the gift or the craftsmanship of the piece or how lucky I was to have a husband who remembered our anniversary, she blurted out, "I guess I won't have to leave you my diamond pin after all." I'll never know exactly what she meant by this but it was hurtful. It was also embarrassing for my husband. I realized then that my mother was a fundamentally unhappy person and I would never be able to share anything with her.

Four years later my mother was diagnosed with leukemia. She was only fifty-five years old. It didn't come as a huge shock since throughout my childhood she had suffered from various ailments. Some of her conditions were real while others I believe were psychosomatic. And others still were illnesses triggered by stress.

My mother did have some real medical problems. She had heart arrhythmia and suffered from palpitations. She was also one of three million people plagued by gastric dumping syndrome, a condition where ingested food bypasses the stomach too quickly and enters the small intestine undigested. Normal digestion time is anywhere from six to eight hours. My mother's food passed within fifteen minutes causing her quite a bit of pain. She also had nausea, bloating, vomiting, and dizziness. This was probably why she was so thin.

My mother was a very smart woman. When she was feeling well she did crossword puzzles and she did them in ink. I have never since seen anyone sit down to do a crossword puzzle with an ink pen. Even when she was well, she didn't do much with her time. She didn't volunteer or give time to charities. She spent most of her free time sleeping. Eventually she had two-thirds of her stomach removed because of an ulcer.

Looking at her through the eyes of a child, I didn't connect the dots. It was much simpler for me then. I liked my friend Nancy's mother better than my own because she lively, attentive, and sweet. She was this tiny woman who let us dress up in all of her clothes. Her shoes were a size three-and-a-half and her evening gowns fit me. She didn't mind one bit every time Nancy and I raided her closet.

I am eleven years older now than my mother lived to be. I see now that my mother held everything in, and the bitterness inside ate her up alive. Going back to her brother, who stole my grandfather's business and reduced them to circumstances in which my grandmother had to clean houses, I can see why she was so angry. I don't think she wanted to be in the meat business, but my Uncle Milton, by the mere virtue of being male, was given an opportunity.

After marrying my father, my mother watched him mismanage their finances. She spent a lifetime trying to be happy from the outside, but nothing was ever enough to fill that gaping hole. I think the hole expanded and filled itself with resentment. It must have also been hard to be dependent on men to take care of her when she was capable and could have taken care of herself.

My mother was treated for her leukemia and went into remission. Shortly after this, she suffered a fall that left her unconscious. She was placed on life support, and her doctor advised me that she most likely had suffered brain damage that would leave her paralyzed on one side of her body.

My mother had wanted a "DO NOT RESUSCITATE" order when she was undergoing cancer treatment, but we never got around to executing it. The doctor treating her for the fall knew her well and talked me through all of the possible outcomes. My mother was very proud, and I knew she wouldn't want to live with one side of her face and body paralyzed. I also knew she wouldn't want to go through chemotherapy again if as a result of the trauma, she fell out of remission.

Through all of this my father was completely shutdown. It fell on me to make the decision to remove my mother from life support. After one long agonizing day, my mother's body finally expired, and she passed away.

Nolan Miller accompanied me to her home to pick out the clothes she would be buried in. We looked everywhere for her false teeth, but they were nowhere to be found. Despite his philandering, it suddenly seemed that my mother was the glue that held my father together. Without her he couldn't function at all.

Tori always brought out the best in my mother. When she was feeling well, we'd stop by for a visit. She had a closet full of toys for Tori that we would pull out and play with. My mother was very natural with her, and even though she never quite seemed to feel the joy of being a grandparent, it was the happiest I ever remember seeing her.

15

Everything's Bigger in Texas

My husband was a dreamer and had been since he was a little boy walking around Dallas, making up stories in his head. When he was about eight years old, Aaron lost use of his legs and was bedridden for a year. His doctors believed it was a form of posttraumatic stress disorder from being bullied on his way to school every day. Aaron was in danger of not being passed onto the next grade. He was required to write twenty-five book reports, and I think he wrote something like one hundred and forty. He probably also came up with countless characters and stories in between book reports. (I once read that film director Martin Scorcese had also been bedridden as a child because of his asthma. He also credits this time with fostering the development of his imagination.)

Aaron was a rugged individualist. An intellectual and creative version, but still, a real "pull-yourself-up-by-the-bootstraps kind of guy." When I think of his vision, his values, his work ethic, and his sense of responsibility, I always think of his roots in the enormous state of Texas. The geography and history of the state were as much a part of my husband's being as his characters were.

Before I met Aaron, I had this notion of Texas being just like it was in the 1956 movie *Giant* starring Rock Hudson, James Dean, and Elizabeth Taylor. These rugged men, their cattle ranches and horses that refused to be tamed. Aaron certainly had the southern drawl but didn't quite fit into the role of Bick or Jett, and he also didn't learn to ride a horse until he came to Los Angeles and got cast in a western.

What I learned over the years from meeting Aaron's family and listening to his stories is that Texas really is the land of the entrepreneurial spirit. Unless you're from Texas, there isn't anyway you would know that, and I found it absolutely fascinating. I never thought about it, but Texas has only four big cities, and the Dallas–Fort Worth area only became a presence in the last twenty or so years. Until then it was Houston and San Antonio, which is funny to think about now because San Antonio is small by today's standards. Other than these four cities, Texas is made up of all these tiny little towns connected by rural highways.

Early in the twentieth century, Texas experienced its oil boom known as "The Gusher Age," when a massive petroleum reserve was discovered near Beaumont. By the 1940s, Texas was the leader of oil production in the United States, and according to some historians, the Texas boom ushered in the global Oil Age. During this rapid forty-year period of development, exploratory wells were drilled all over Texas. Wildcatters were the adventurous entrepreneurs who jumped in their trucks and went from place to place drilling wells in areas not known to be oil fields. The term evolved from the wells that were drilled out in the middle of nowhere, where only wildcats lived. Many of these wildcatters made their fortunes, but they started out with very humble beginnings.

In his own way, Aaron was a wildcatter who struck oil in Hollywood. He had the vision, the imagination, and the drive. Aaron became Aaron Spelling not just because he was such a prolific writer but also because, true to his

Texas roots, he wanted to be a stakeholder in his own ideas and play an active role in the creative process. He was already a successful writer at Four Star Entertainment. Many writers would have been satisfied with that alone. Aaron was different. He wanted to find his own well. That Texas spirit of entrepreneurship was hardwired into him. He wanted his own land, and he wanted to be his own oil well.

Vanity Fair columnist Dominick Dunne, who had known Aaron since the mid-1950s, once touted, "I can honestly say that I'm one of the few people who remember him from when he was poor." Dunne added, "From the time he started making money, Aaron always lived in big houses." As a Texan, the ultimate symbol of Aaron's success would have been a ranch in West Texas. It's where tycoons (and former presidents) historically go to disconnect from the world, ride their horses, and sit on the porch. I suppose this is what was in the back of Aaron's mind when we moved from our 2,500-square-foot house off Coldwater Canyon to our 6,500-square-foot house on Palm Drive in Beverly Hills. From here we moved to a 12,000-square-foot house right on the corner on North Mapleton Drive and Sunset Boulevard in Holmby Hills. Aaron's motivation at the time was a sandbox he had bought for Tori. He didn't think it fit properly in the backyard of the Beverly Hills House, so we moved to a neighborhood where the homes had more land around them.

At that point, a third of ABC-TV's primetime lineup was made up of Aaron's shows. *The Love Boat, Fantasy Island, Dynasty,* and *Hotel,* just to name a few. I think in Aaron's mind it was time to buy his West Texas ranch. The only thing was that he wanted it to be in Los Angeles. I couldn't believe it, but Aaron was very serious about buying a third home where, in addition to all the pets we already had, we could add farm animals. Aaron did most of his writing in bed surrounded by our dogs, so now I was picturing him like Dr. Dolittle in bed with dogs, goats, chickens, and piglets, polishing a script.

Tori and Aaron really were kindred spirits when it came to animals, so she couldn't have been any more excited. She wanted the ranch more than anything. I had negotiated a deal with Tori whereby we would rehome her turtle and she would be allowed to add yet another dog to our pack. That was how I kept our numbers down. Aaron obviously didn't remember our Easter bunny fiasco. The kids couldn't handle cleaning out two bunny cages. Imagine what would happen with a barn full of farm animals. They would definitely be more difficult to return than a pair of bunnies.

The truth is that with so many of his shows shooting simultaneously, Aaron wasn't home much, and he also didn't have much responsibility with the day-to-day management of the house, the kids, or our second home in Malibu. All of that was exclusively my responsibility. I was very involved with my children's schools—one day I was in class making dioramas, and the next I was leading a troop of Brownies in arts and crafts. All of this, while being Wife-in-Chief running the hospitality and special events division of Aaron Spelling Productions.

I knew that in the late 1930s, Barbara Stanwyck had built an eleven-acre ranch out in Northridge so she could raise horses. The property included an equestrian facility and a beautifully designed twelve-bedroom house that had a stunning stone veneer and charming wooden shingles. Even though she remodeled it and merged it with her friend and neighbor Zeppo Marx's property, Barbara ended up selling it after marrying actor Robert Taylor. The driving distance to the Hollywood community where they both worked proved to be too far from Northridge. This was back when Van Nuys was considered rural and the post office only had forty residents listed in the area, so imagine the commute in 1980s traffic.

I loved animals then as I do now, and I was the kind of wife and mom who wanted her family to have everything their hearts desired. But honestly, Aaron wasn't thinking it through. As usual, he was leaving everything practical to me. A working ranch meant ranch hands, ranch hands meant a ranch manager, and a ranch manager meant another house on the property for the ranch manager. The mere thought of it was enough to put me over the edge. I felt like Eva Gabor in *Green Acres,* only this episode wasn't a comedy.

I knew Aaron wasn't going to take no for an answer, just like he didn't believe me when I said Tori's sandbox would fit into the yard of our home on Palm Drive. This, by the way, was also an early case of "good cop" (Aaron) and "bad cop" (me), so I needed to find a solution. I gave it some thought, and when I felt like I had the answer, I called a family meeting in my office. The idea that I ultimately proposed was that instead of buying a third house, we put our existing house on the market and find a new house that would combine the city living we were already enjoying with the country life we wanted.

Aaron and the kids were skeptical of my proposal, but I knew my plan was feasible. I elaborated on how I thought it could work and assured the kids that yes, really, they would be able to have all the animals they wanted. I couldn't help but think of the irony that my mother wouldn't let me have pets and told me I could have as many as I wanted once I was married. Now here I was with a husband and two children who were animal obsessed. Everyone knew to call us if a family dog wasn't "working out."

After I outlined my plan for more space and hence more animals, all the Spellings said "aye." With my mission accomplished, the meeting was adjourned, and I retired to my bathroom for a relaxing bath. In those days, this was the only place I had any privacy. Even with the scented candles and the aromatherapy bath salts, the release of tension was only temporary. I had my marching orders and without haste would have to find houses for my husband the wildcatter to look at.

16

There Goes the Neighborhood

Like any other family, we hired a Realtor and explained the kind of house we were interested in finding. It actually wasn't that tall an order. Many people don't realize that Los Angeles is an expansive city with rustic areas. I think most visitors only think of the historic Santa Monica Pier, Rodeo Drive, Hollywood, and of course Disneyland. There are areas like Mandeville Canyon, which known for its sycamore trees, oak trees, and horse-friendly hiking trails. Robert Mitchum, Esther Williams, Eva Marie Saint, and Aaron's former boss Dick Powell were just a few of the people who lived out in the canyon. There were also some unique country-style properties up at the top of Coldwater Canyon near Mulholland Drive. These were properties left over from the horse-and-buggy days my mother talked about. The houses were small, but the wilderness around the houses had somehow been left largely unspoiled.

Just across Sunset Boulevard, and only a couple of miles from our home on North Mapleton Drive, was what was known as "Bing Crosby's old estate." It was on South Mapleton and Club View Drives, right across the street from Holmby Park, which is known for its 18-hole pitch-and-putt golf course and its lawn bowling court. It was a very charming neighborhood.

Built in the 1930s, the house was perched atop a knoll with a panoramic view of Los Angeles. The vista included an expanse from downtown Los Angeles to Catalina Island. I'm not sure why it was called "Bing Crosby's old estate." Bing had lived there from 1943 to 1964, but it had been just over twenty years since he had owned it. Malcolm McNaghten was the original owner of the land and had the house built in 1932.

A Los Angeles businessman, McNaghten was given the land by his father-in-law Arthur Letts, who was the founder of Broadway Department Store and Bullock's. He was the first Anglo owner of what was known as the Wolfskill Ranch, which was part of one of the early California ranchos. Letts developed his acreage into what would become Westwood and Holmby Hills.

In 1932, McNaghten retained the services of architect Gordon B. Kaufmann, who also designed oil tycoon E. L. Doheny's landmark Greystone Estate in Beverly Hills, to design his home. At the time, the United States was in the middle of the Great Depression, so McNaghten's decision to begin construction on his 15,000-square-foot mega mansion was scrutinized, but he forged ahead with his plans. Other members of the community saw the project as a source of employment for skilled laborers and a hopeful symbol that perhaps the economy was turning around.

McNaghten lived in the house until 1943, when he sold it to actor Bing Crosby and his wife, Dixie Lee Crosby. Crosby had just made news for what was called his "White Hot Christmas" in which his Toluca Lake Mansion was ravaged by a fire caused by faulty wiring that ignited the family's dry, brittle Christmas tree. Bing sold his Toluca Lake colonial and moved into the Holmby Hills house with Dixie Lee and their four sons. Unfortunately, Dixie passed away in 1952 after a bout with cancer, but Bing and the four sons remained there. Bing remarried Kathryn Grant and had three more children with her.

In 1964, Bing sold the house to Patrick J. Frawley for a reported $350,000. Frawley was the president of the Schick Safety Razor Company. He was also the founder of the Schick Treatment Centers. On his website, *Paradise Leased*, historian Steve Vaught writes, "According to Hedda Hopper, when Crosby departed he left behind a keg of red wine in the home's basement. A few months later, Frawley checked himself into the Schadel Hospital to cure himself of alcoholism. Coincidence? Hmmm. Frawley's ultimately successful treatment led him to buy Schadel Hospital and open up a series [of] Schick Alcoholic Treatment centers. So shouldn't Bing be thanked for that?'"

The fact that Bing Crosby had kept a petting zoo on the property seemed like kismet. There was a little creek and what looked like dens built by otters on the creek. We knew instinctively that this was our new home. In 1986, we paid $10,250,000 for the house and five acres. We later learned that the monkeys Bing kept in cages on the back of the property were rumored to be his primitive home security system. Their screeching was apparently enough to send any intruder—or neighbor, for the matter—running for the hills.

We shot video of the property before breaking ground on our remodel in 1988. Our friend Phyllis George, who was co-anchor of *The Early Show* on CBS at the time, was the on-scene reporter as Aaron and I ceremoniously tossed the first chunk of dirt with a shovel. It was not in our collective minds that day to break the Greystone Estate's record as the largest residence in Los Angeles at 46,000 square feet. Our original intention was just to update the kitchen and the bathrooms, take away some of the old nooks and crannies, and add rooms here and there. When both the builder and the architect, James Langenheim, recommended that we simply raze the original 1932 construction and start from scratch, we quickly became familiarized with a stanza from Scottish poet Robert Burns's poem *To a Mouse,*

In proving foresight may be vain:
The best laid schemes of mice and men,
Go often awry,
And leave us nothing but grief and pain,
For promised joy!

The poem may have been written in 1785, but it definitely applied to our remodel two hundred years later. Unfortunately, we weren't the only ones feeling the pain. Some of our new neighbors were not happy and made it very clear. They say truth is stranger than fiction, and it really was.

Our neighbor across the street was outside every morning in her kaftan waiting for the construction company to arrive. She made a big show of counting all the construction trucks, and then she'd run up her driveway and call the city. Meanwhile, our neighbors right next door to us on Club View who never so much as spoke a word to us launched a seven-year offensive against us. It was seven years of measuring our fences with yardsticks and running a ruler against the property line trying to catch us in violation by even centimeters. Strangely enough, the husband was a very successful television director who was about Aaron's age, so they had probably come up the ranks together. Surely he could have picked up the phone and called Aaron. It would have been easy enough.

Even though our kids went to the same schools, we never crossed paths. Her frustrations with us came via neighbors and of course via our contractor. We wrote one check after another to them in hopes of appeasing them, but it never seemed to be enough. I think we finally gave up worrying about them when we heard through the grapevine that our plan to put up gates around our property was very upsetting to them. Theirs was the only house that didn't have gates, and we were somehow tarnishing the image of the neighborhood. I had to laugh; these were all multi-, multimillion dollar homes, and she was trying to stand on the principle of false humility.

Neither Aaron nor I ever thought about the consequences that would ensue when we tore down the original house and started construction on the new one.

It wasn't just the neighbors. There was quite a bit of public scrutiny as well, including that of the *Los Angeles Times,* which chronicled the construction of the house. In April of 1988, Jeannine Stein, a reporter for the *LA Times,* wrote an article called "The House of Spelling: Massive Construction Project in Holmby Hills Flusters Some Neighbors." This was the reporter's lead:

"What's bigger than a football field, smaller than Hearst Castle, has a bowling alley and an entire floor of closets, and is making some people very annoyed? Aaron and Candy Spelling's 56,500-square-foot mansion in Holmby Hills. The French chateau, under construction now for two years, has turned the corner of Mapleton and Club View drives into a gawker's paradise. Sprawled across 6 acres on what once was the Bing Crosby estate, the house dwarfs the sizable mansions on the block and looms large over tranquil Holmby Park near Wilshire Boulevard."

Our neighbor who counted the trucks, whom we'd never met (and never did), went on record in the article:

"Audrey Irmas, who lives across the street, won an injunction against the television producer and the construction company three years ago. She calls the house, which obscures her view of the sunrise, "Look-at-me-I'm-rich architecture."

'I hope I never lay eyes on them,' she adds."

I understood neighbors wanting to limit construction hours and being concerned about the congestion caused by the heavy construction vehicles. I never understood, however, why they made it so personal. Even after our neighbor had gotten her injunction and we complied with the modified construction hours, she continued waging her war in the press. The Kansas-based *Lawrence Journal World* ran a feature called "Is Bigger Really Better in the Land of Conspicuous Consumption?" In this piece she referred to our house as a "mental institution."

The only good news about this article was that the reporter, Jeff Wilson of the Associated Press, also got the other side of the story. The late Elaine Young, who was known as the Realtor to the stars, went on record, "That's nothing. . . . The biggest monument is going to be by the Sultan of Brunei behind the Beverly Hills Hotel. He's torn down five houses for a palace."

It's true, the house grew beyond the original scope, but we were in compliance with all of the city's laws and building codes, so we didn't give much thought to it. We had a wonderful architect and his design was proportional, and even at 56,000 square feet, the house didn't occupy more than 50 percent of the property. Our perspective was pretty simple. Aaron's hard work and perseverance had finally paid off. His career had spiraled upward. The poor Jewish kid from Texas who came to Los Angeles with borrowed money could afford to build his dream house complete with a bowling alley and a barbershop. The man who refused to ever get on a plane was creating his version of his West Texas ranch where he could bowl with his family and friends (Aaron's version of horseback riding), sit on the front porch, and host his traditional Sunday night barbecues.

I won't lie. Working on the interior design of the house was every woman's dream. I took two different ten-day trips to France and England to choose fabrics and furniture, and I also bought my fireplaces there. I remember sometimes going into Aaron's office, and he was on the phone with someone at the network. I would try to get his attention to show him swatches of fabric or pieces of tile and stone, but he wasn't even remotely interested. While he was dialing his next phone call, he would take a minute with me.

"I need to pay for this house. It's up to you to build it. Whatever you want is always perfect." So while Aaron continued creating television shows, I built the house.

It took a crew of one hundred and fifty men, five hundred tons of steel, one hundred seventy thousand glass tiles for the swimming pool, and two hundred thousand hand-laid granite pavers. Our foyer was made complete with the *Gone with the Wind*–inspired double-sided spiral staircase. And yes, it was imported from none other than Texas and brought in and installed in one continuous piece. It was Tori who christened the house "The Manor." We did other fun things like have a small kitchenette installed in the master bedroom where we could microwave popcorn for watching movies in bed or prepare snacks. I also hand-drew a floral pattern that we had reproduced and used as a motif throughout the master bedroom.

One of my favorite rooms in the house (besides my fantasy bathroom, which is really my sanctuary) was Aaron's study. This was a room that I put extra care into. I really wanted it to reflect his talent and his accomplishments. It had majestic wood paneling, a magnificent oversized desk, and enough shelf space to hold his bound leather scripts with gilded font on the spine, until he was one hundred and eight years old. Aaron didn't write in this room, but it was where he held all of his important meetings.

In the end The Manor was 56,500 square feet, which did not include our 17,000-square-foot attic. The attic was like our own personal warehouse. It's where we stored our luggage for all of our old-fashioned train trips across the country. It housed all of our decorations for every holiday. I still can't believe this nice Jewish girl decorated her house for Christmas, but I really did love all of the lights and the ornaments. I still get wistful thinking about it. The attic also had space for my collectibles, which are numerous.

We moved in on Valentine's Day 1991. Even on this day that is supposed to be about friendship and love, our next-door neighbor was still at it and would be for quite some time. I'm not sure how many months or years later, but I was out walking our property one day and something got into me. I picked up some rotten fruit that had fallen off of our trees and threw it over the fence into her yard. I know it was naughty, but sometimes a girl's got to do what a girl's got to do.

The *Los Angeles Times* was also not done with us. In a review of The Manor, contributor Sam Hall Kaplan called it one of the worst architectural projects of the '80s:

"Aaron Spelling residence, which at 56,500 square feet, should be considered a congregate living facility and not a single-family home, and therefore in violation of Holmby Hills zoning. What Spelling's folly is, of course, is a sad commentary on the distorted values that have taken the architectural form of monster mansions at a time when tens of thousands of persons are homeless."

And even when Aaron passed away, *The New York Times* printed this as part of his obituary, "Mr. Spelling himself, though a self-effacing and extremely shy man in private, put his own vast wealth on display in the late 1980s when he and his wife, Candy, supervised the construction of their home in the Holmby Hills section of Los Angeles. The structure, which like his shows drew mostly scathing reviews, eventually contained 123 rooms over about 56,000 square feet. It was said to include a bowling alley, an ice rink and an entire wing devoted to his wife's wardrobe."

If any, I think I my only regret is that we were somewhat apologetic all these years for having built The Manor. Especially now in light of the Bernie Madoff scandal, I feel that I should have stood up and reminded people that Aaron earned every last cent. He didn't embezzle it from anyone and then abscond with it. He was the most prolific television writer-producer in the world. He still holds the Guinness World Record as the most prolific producer. Even though he's been gone for seven years, he is still ranked in the top twelve posthumously earning celebrities. He was also incredibly generous, whether it was with the writers he hired on his shows or with charities he supported financially.

I feel like I also should have spoken up on behalf of my gift-wrapping room. For years now it has been fodder for every media outlet and comedy sketch show. Practically speaking, we sent out literally thousands of gifts to network executives, agents, talent managers, writers, producers, celebrities, stylists, heads of state—this list goes on. It doesn't even include friends and family. It wasn't as if I was buying gifts for myself all day and then wrapping them for myself.

What most people don't know about me is that I'm actually very creative. After my divorce from Howard, I enrolled at the Chouinard design school. So for me, designing, packaging, and wrapping the gifts is an art. I notice nobody gives Martha Stewart or Rosie O'Donnell any grief for their much-publicized crafting rooms, but somehow I get it all.

Despite all this negativity, we've also had fun with some of the attention. John Perry, a singer I'd never heard of, composed the Calypso song "The

Ballad of Aaron and Candy (An Ode to Spelling's Dwelling)" which I have yet
to hear. I was able to find the lyrics online:

> "See Candy's jewels, see Aaron's money,
> Aaron doesn't think being picked on is funny.
> See Candy's clothes, see Aaron's pad
> See Aaron and Candy's castle make the neighbors mad.
> But they're livin' in splendor high above the crowds
> 60,000 square feet of heaven.
> That's Spelling's dwelling, I said
> Spelling's Dwelling. . . ."

In the movie *Legally Blonde,* Elle Woods played by Reese Witherspoon
described her social standing to Warner Huntington III by saying "I grew up in
Bel Air, Warner. Across the street from Aaron Spelling." It was an unexpected
homage, and both Aaron and I got a kick out of it. I can only imagine what our
neighbors must have thought.

17

The Entertainers

They came every three minutes starting in the early morning until the wee hours of the night. Some were topless. Some looked like they were going on safari. There was one in particular that was very somber and sent shivers up our spines. We could never understand what they were saying, but the cadence of their respective voices was always the same. One night, Aaron hopped onto a big red double-decker that looked as if it had come straight from London. It was stopped right in front of our gates just as we were returning from an evening out. It really threw me for a loop to see Aaron on board the Hollywood tour bus. The passengers were literally gasping. For that matter, so was I.

I couldn't help smiling as my husband made his way down the aisle. He was smiling, shaking everybody's hands, and of course, talking. When he got back in the car, I asked him what he had said. He told me that he had thanked everyone for watching his shows over the years and for helping us build our dream home. The fans on that bus represented almost every one of his shows: *Fantasy Island, Dynasty, Beverly Hills 90210, Starsky and Hutch,* and *Melrose Place.*

That was Aaron. He had his very humble beginnings but never forgot them and never took anything for granted. I loved the quality of his character from the very first time I met him. And that generous and open spirit really was what our home was about.

There is no doubt The Manor became a stage for legendary parties where we hosted movie stars, television stars, royalty, heads of state, and the biggest players in finance. My mother would have been pleased that everything she had worked so hard to instill in me had turned out to be of great value.

It sounds funny to say, but we really were just a regular family living at The Manor, and our days in that respect were quite ordinary. Aaron was always up early and went downstairs to have his breakfast and tea in the Breakfast Room. Then he'd come back upstairs to dress and was off to work either on set or at his office. He worked very long days. Our children went to school, and afterward they usually did their homework in my office, where I worked on projects for my charities and our foundations. When Aaron came home at night, he usually had the phone glued to his ear until we sat down to dinner.

I always stayed up later than Aaron did. Sometimes I would bake and other times I would do things like work on my scrapbooks. Another thing I absolutely loved to do was just relax in my bathroom. I would take baths or give myself an in-home minifacial. This was truly the only room where I had any privacy, so when we built the house, I had a chaise put in there so I could really relax.

When the kids were teenagers, they had all their friends over to the house. I preferred our house being the "hang out." This way I always knew what was going on. My kids were typical teenagers. I liked their friends but knew I had to keep an eye on them. One time I caught one of them drinking a screwdriver. It looked like just an ordinary glass of orange juice, but I had a feeling it wasn't, and I was right.

On the weekends Aaron and Randy played tennis. We also had friends over to bowl. One of my favorite things to do was have movie night at our house with a small group of good friends. I'd set out desserts in our screening room, and we'd watch the latest attraction.

For more formal occasions, our dining room table seated thirty people. I always had French service with a butler at either end of the table. This allowed everyone to be served at the same time. I had every accessory imaginable. My sterling silver was kept in a humidity-controlled room, and our collection of wines was stored in a temperature-controlled cellar.

To this day, people e-mail me or stop me on the street to ask for tips about hosting everything from bridal showers to holiday dinners. I have to say, I have acquired quite a bit of wisdom over the years, starting with the first barbecue I hosted at Aaron's house the weekend that I met him. The first thing I always tell anyone who asks is that the most important element to a successful party is creating a welcoming atmosphere where everyone feels comfortable.

When I think of all the celebrations we hosted at The Manor, one of the best ones was the Easter party we organized for Centro de Niños, a nonprofit bilingual and bicultural day-care center. Centro de Niños serves the working poor in East Los Angeles. For years, we hosted an Easter celebration just for them on Good Friday. Our guest list included somewhere between one hundred and fifty to two hundred children.

The looks on their faces when they arrived and saw the decorations, the moon bounces, and the stage for the puppet show were just amazing. It was sort of heartbreaking and heartwarming all at once. I'll never forget seeing all those pairs of shoes lined up in front of the moon bounces. I thought, how are these kids going to remember where they left their shoes? Somehow they always did.

We put a lot of effort into creating handmade Easter baskets, complete with an Easter bunny, for every one of the children. This was back before the candy companies manufactured the plastic eggs with the candy already inside of them, so we were usually up until three or four in the morning assembling the plastic eggs and wrapping the baskets in my gift-wrapping room.

The Easter baskets were always a big hit, and they really made staying up all night worth it. We also made a tradition of bringing the kids up to the doll room so they could see my collection of Madame Alexander dolls. It was like a trip to a toy museum for them, and they really enjoyed it.

I became involved with the Centro de Niños at the suggestion of Richard Alatorre, who was a city councilman in Los Angeles. Richard was one of the most influential Latinos in the state of California and among other things, he was an important advocate for children in the community of East Los Angeles.

After moving into The Manor, we had many requests to hold fund-raisers there, but we were always very selective. I really wanted to support a children's charity. We had a short list and met with three of four different charities before meeting with Sandra Serrano-Sewell, the executive director of Centro de Niños. After just five minutes with her, I knew I wanted to be involved with them.

One of my biggest fund-raisers for Centro de Niños was from my QVC Madame Alexander doll collection. In 1994, my longtime friend Nolan Miller was at QVC selling them some jewelry he had designed. He happened to see some dolls from a doll collection they were considering, and he told them very unapologetically, "The dolls are ugly." He suggested they speak with me about creating a doll collection for them. By then I had been a collector of Madame Alexander dolls for about fifteen years. Not long after, the president of QVC, Doug Briggs, asked me to do a collection for them.

It goes without saying that the idea of introducing a whole line of my own beautiful fantasy dolls was thrilling, but I also knew how much work and time would be involved. Aaron and the kids were always my number-one priority. Even though Tori and Randy were teenagers by then, I knew my husband needed to be part of the decision. It was going to be a tough sell because taking this on would require at least two trips to New York City and at least a year, if not more, of preparation.

My proposal to embark on this project went over with Aaron like a lead balloon. We had a very traditional marriage, and Aaron never liked it when I wasn't available to him or to make decisions for the kids. I still hadn't traveled anywhere without him in all the time that we had been married. It took me about a week, but I was finally able to convince my husband that this was a huge opportunity for me. I argued that the president of QVC had asked me himself, and Madame Alexander wanted to produce my designs.

Once Aaron got on board, he was very supportive. I flew to New York City to the Madame Alexander factory in Harlem, which had once been the original factory for Dodge. After meeting with executives at Madame Alexander, we flew to Westchester, Pennsylvania, to meet with Doug Briggs and the business affairs attorney for QVC. I told them both that one of my requirements was that my profits and proceeds would be donated to Centro de Niños.

Once I had the green light from my husband and QVC, I set up a workshop in the attic of The Manor. I was literally up there with the dustpans, cleaning supplies, and all of our vacuums. That was where I put together my ideas and sketched out each doll. I tacked up my swatches and also had photographic references. It was such an exciting time. I was so inspired while I was working on the collection. I knew the back story of each doll and exactly what every one should look like down to the smallest detail.

It took a year and a half to complete the collection of twenty-four dolls. There were two sizes: twelve-inch and seventeen-inch. All the dolls had different hairdos and fabulous underpinnings. The time just flew, and before I knew it, it was time to fly back to New York City for the big day. Like any designer, I was so proud of my work, especially in light of how much sacrifice had gone into it. On Sunday, September 18, 1994, we went on the air during prime time for three hours. It was a win-win situation for me, QVC, and of course all the children at the Centro de Niños.

The other fund-raiser that is most memorable in my mind happens to have followed on the heels of my QVC venture. It seems funny to call it a fund-raiser since it was a dinner with Prince Charles, but the evening was in fact an event to raise funds for his charitable foundation, The Prince's Charities. Lew and Edie Wasserman asked Aaron and me to host the dinner for the Prince of Wales, who was on a goodwill tour following his divorce from Diana, Princess of Wales.

We agreed to it without having any idea of what was involved. The guest list was a real "Who's Who" of Hollywood with plates going for $10,000 each.

After all the RSVPs were accounted for, the list was about three hundred people long. About a week before Prince Charles was scheduled to arrive, an advance team came out to meet with us.

The advance party included a press secretary, logistics manager, senior personnel in charge of security, and a researcher. They briefed us on royal etiquette, outlined the proper table setting, and helped us create a menu that would be to the Prince's liking. We learned quickly that royal appearances are tightly scripted and that there is not much room for improvisation.

First and most important was the "no-touch" rule. Even if Prince Charles were to show us or any of our guests attention, we were not to make the mistake of reaching out and touching him. If the Prince happened to extend his hand, we were supposed to deviate from our American custom of shaking his hand. Instead, we were instructed to touch it very lightly and very briefly.

The second rule was that nobody could be seated at dinner until Prince Charles was seated. Then everyone else could take their places at their respective tables. Part and parcel of this rule was the protocol that we were to stop eating if the Prince stopped eating. I didn't see how this could work unless everybody stared at the Prince all through dinner. Finally, and this was the hardest one for Aaron, nobody was allowed to get up from the dinner table until the Prince did.

I honestly thought finding a caterer to prepare game bird for three hundred people was going to be the biggest challenge. The evening was going to be very complex, and because I am such a perfectionist, it was absolutely nerve-wracking. The logistics manager did a walk-through of the house with me, and we worked out where the dinner would be held. There would be tents outside and guests would walk through the house.

The trouble with the plan as outlined was that we were going to have three hundred pairs of shoes walking over my light-colored silk carpets. Prince or no Prince, this didn't work for me. I knew my gorgeous silk carpets would never survive. The solution we came up with was that the room would be carpeted with an area carpet, at the expense of the Prince. So days before the dinner, a carpet company came and installed a light-colored carpet in what I came to call the "Prince Charles Suite" of The Manor.

The night of the fund-raiser arrived and so did Prince Charles along with his entourage that included more than one valet. He was a nice man, very soft-spoken. I hadn't smoked in years, but that night I went off and had a cigarette by myself to calm my nerves.

We took the Prince into Aaron's office, where his valets straightened everything from his tie to his shoelaces. When one of the valets accidentally dropped a cuff link, everyone on the Prince's team fell to their hands and knees to look for it. It was clear that Aaron and I were expected to do the same. So we did. I still have this image of Aaron rolling his eyes at me as we combed through the carpet fibers looking for the Prince's cuff link.

The dinner went off without a hitch. I was seated next to the Prince, and I think because I was the hostess (though my girlfriends say it's because I was his type), he was very focused on having a conversation with me. We talked about his sons, William and Harry. He was also interested in architecture, so we chatted about the L'oiseau-style architecture of The Manor and also some restoration projects he supported through his charity fund. By the time we moved on to the dessert course, I could tell Aaron was desperate to sneak off and go to bed.

Finally, dinner was over and the Prince stood up. He was very polite and offered us thanks as we escorted him to his waiting car. As the motorcade pulled past our gates, Aaron sighed with relief.

"I thought he'd never leave."

18

Upstairs Downstairs

The Prince of Wales wasn't our only houseguest from the House of Windsor. We actually had a couple others. My friend Edie Goetz was the daughter of Louis B. Mayer. She had an exquisite art collection that included Picasso's *Motherhood* painting from his Blue Period. Edie also had a butler named Lodge. Having been footman to the Queen Mother before coming to Los Angeles, he was a treasure in his own right. Lodge worked for Edie until she passed away in 1988, at which point he returned to London.

While we were building The Manor, I had become somewhat friendly with David Geffen, known to all as the wealthiest man in entertainment. In 1990, David made headlines when he purchased the 9.4-acre Jack Warner Estate on Angelo Drive in Beverly Hills for $47.5 million. At the time this was the highest price paid in the United States for a private home. David started his remodel on the Warner estate about a year before we moved into The Manor.

When The Manor was complete and became the center of so much media attention, I received an inquiry from Lodge the butler. He was seeking employment. Butlers with credentials were not easy to come by in Hollywood, so I immediately offered him a job.

Lodge flew out and became part of our staff. He was absolutely wonderful. He really had this regal air about him. We loved hearing all the stories about the royal family, and we also learned the differences between butlers and housemen—butlers don't clean. One day David called to tell me he was putting French limestone on the terraces of the estate. Lodge was in the background as I gave David my honest opinion.

"No, don't do that! The limestone is going to crack. I've already had to replace some stones." David told me that his interior designer Rose Tarlow had already ordered the limestone. He didn't think he could change course at this stage of the game.

About a year later, David had finally finished his remodel. The house was done and he was moving in. Just days later, my security personnel informed me that Lodge was gone.

"What do you mean he's gone?" I asked. Apparently Lodge had literally packed his suitcase at two or three in the morning and fled. I couldn't imagine where he had gone.

"He went to work for David Geffen."

I couldn't believe what I was hearing. My security team explained that Lodge had been offered a job by David Geffen but didn't have the courage to face me, so he had run off in the middle of the night.

A few months later, Lodge's best friend, James, came to work for us. He had also worked at Kensington Palace. I guess we didn't interview him thoroughly enough because one evening when Tori had some friends over for a Murder Mystery party, James told me with disdain that he didn't serve children. Needless to say, James didn't last long as a member of our staff. A few years later when Tori was on *Beverly Hills 90210*, Aaron was also promoting his book *A Prime-Time Life*. Aaron had a book signing at Book Soup on the Sunset Strip so we went as family. I couldn't believe it, but there was none other than James waiting in line. When he got up to the table, he asked if he could take a picture with Tori. I found it very curious that James wouldn't wait on her at the house but had no problem waiting in a long line to get her autograph now that she was on a hit television show.

We went through another couple of English butlers before I finally figured out that they all left as soon as they got their Green Card. We also received applications from several other butlers with resumés that included experience at Kensington Palace. It turned out to be easy enough to check references at the palace, and let's just say a number of those applicants didn't check out.

Sometimes our personnel issue at The Manor involved staff members who wouldn't leave. For eighteen years we employed a housekeeper named Mrs. Hing. We called her Hing for short. She started working for us when she was close to the age when most people are thinking about retirement. Hing became one of our live-in housekeepers who stayed overnight five days a week. She had a bedroom in The Manor with a nice bed, a dresser, a club chair, and other accessories. Her work ethic was unbelievable especially considering her age.

When she wasn't sleeping at The Manor, Hing stayed with her daughter, Suzi. Well, one day I happened to be in the motor court when Hing's daughter came to pick her up. She was driving a massive Cadillac Escalade with those fancy rims and what appeared to be a custom mesh grill. It looked like something you'd see on one of those MTV reality shows. Hing looked over at me with such an expression of scorn her face.

"I paid for that car."

Years later when I was thinking about selling The Manor, I thought it would be the perfect time to retire Hing. She was 84 years old and quite honestly, I was very worried about her health. So we offered her a nice severance package that she accepted, and then she retired.

Not a week later Hing called. She needed a job. This time she was more clear. She needed a job to support her daughter. I didn't know what to say to her, but I knew offering her a job was not the answer. I thought it would be a nice gesture to let Hing have some of the furnishings from her room. I thought perhaps the club chair, the dresser, or her nightstand might be comforting for her to have in her room at her daughter's house. She was very appreciative of the offer and said she would make arrangements to come by.

Well, it was Hing's daughter who came by in her Escalade. She also brought a second car driven by a friend. They took every piece of furniture and bedding from Hing's old room. The literally stripped the room bare and loaded up the cars with everything except for the headboard that was mounted on the wall.

Sometimes I find myself thinking about Hing. I hope retirement is treating her well. I also still think about Lodge. I wonder, was The Manor just too much work, or were we not high enough on the Social Register for him?

19

The Story of the Storyteller

Aaron always used to tease me and tell me I was the worst storyteller. I always knew that if I forgot an important detail and then went back to it, or waited too long to deliver the punch line, my husband the raconteur was bound to give me a bad review. "Candy, you are the worst storyteller." Throughout our marriage when we went to formal dinner parties or big Hollywood events, it was always my job to make sure Aaron and I looked good. It was his job to do the talking.

This arrangement worked for me then because I was still a little shy, and those evenings could be overwhelming. With my loquacious husband at my side, I always had the comfort of knowing that he would get other people talking. I know my storytelling ability is not as bad as he made it out to be; it's just that I don't tell stories the way Aaron did, but then again, who could?

Aaron's repeated bouts with cancer and his subsequent struggle with Alzheimer's is not a story he would be able to tell. This would be the one story in which Aaron would gloss over important facts, skip ahead, and diminish the impact of the central theme. It is a difficult tale to tell, but I am the only one who can tell it because I was there at his side throughout it all.

In the early 1990s, Aaron was diagnosed with prostate cancer. He had a successful surgery and was given a clean bill of health. A few years later, it must have been around 2000, he developed a cough that just wouldn't go away. We went to see our family ENT doctor, who made the initial diagnosis.

Aaron was a tobacco pipe smoker and had a collection of about six hundred Dunhill and Sasieni 4 Dot pipes. He amassed this collection because he would smoke each one only between twenty and thirty times and then was done with it. When he posed for portraits for the television network, he insisted on being photographed with his trusty pipe. I came to know more about pipes than I ever thought I would because of Aaron. I learned how much tobacco to put in them to break them in and the different kinds of mouthpieces available. Aaron preferred the fishtail because he liked to hold the pipe in his mouth when he was working.

It used to really worry me to see the pipe just hanging on his lips. I couldn't help but say something to him. We must have had the same conversation a million times. He would tell me he wasn't inhaling and then I would point out that it didn't matter, his mouth was still full of hot tobacco smoke.

Our ENT accompanied us to see the oncologist at UCLA. The strange thing about this particular appointment was that when the oncologist was verbally going through Aaron's medical history with him, he asked him whether he had any history of cancer.

"No."

I jumped in to correct my husband, "That's not true. You had prostate cancer." I was never quite sure if Aaron was intentionally revising his medical history or whether he edited that time from his memory the same way he edited out scenes from his scripts. In either case I knew I could never let him go to the doctor alone again.

Based on Aaron's symptoms and an examination, the oncologist at UCLA was 99 percent certain Aaron had throat cancer. It was grim but not surprising. It was everything I feared all those years that Aaron's Dunhill pipe sat in his mouth. The only thing more frightening than the diagnosis was the recommended treatment. The doctor believed that the only way to treat the throat cancer was to remove three quarters of Aaron's tongue. Aaron said he would rather die than let them cut out his tongue.

Somehow I managed to stay out of the emotion of the situation. There was no biopsy yet, so really we didn't know exactly what we were dealing with. I believed there would be a better answer if we took the next step of having the biopsy performed. It would be at least a week before it could be done because even for this they needed to make sure Aaron was in good health. When the day arrived, we had the biopsy done and then headed out to Malibu. I'll never forget our housekeeper erupting into hysteria when Aaron lit up his pipe at the beach house.

"Mrs. Spelling! Mrs. Spelling! He's smoking again!" Our staff was crazy about Aaron and they didn't want to see anything happen to him. None of us did.

Somewhere I had heard the expression, "Man can live forty days without food, three days without water, and about eight minutes without air . . . but not one minute without hope." When the biopsy came back positive for cancer, I knew I had to keep hope alive. This was definitely our darkest hour. I had never dealt with oncologists before but somehow I figured out how to tackle it. I ordered slides of the biopsy and then called every leading cancer center in the country to let them know I was sending them. I had phone consultations and prayed that Aaron wouldn't need to travel somewhere far away for treatment because I knew we'd have to take a train. The cancer was aggressive and we didn't have the luxury of time.

Coincidentally, we ended up less than ten miles away at St. John's Hospital in Santa Monica. The doctor there was confident Aaron's cancer could be successfully treated with treatment and technology that UCLA did not offer because it was a teaching school. This particular external radiation machine was called an IMRT machine. It allowed the doctor to pinpoint the dose of radiation delivered in the body with greater precision than ever before. This reduced side effects and protected the healthy tissue in the body. The treatment required that Aaron be fitted for a face mask and a mouth brace so his teeth wouldn't fall out. It was a lot of information to process. Ultimately, we decided this was the path we would take.

The next six weeks were quite an ordeal for both of us. I could see that just preparing mentally for the treatment really took it out of Aaron. We were at the hospital almost every day, and when we weren't there, we were at home bracing ourselves for the next round of radiation. Oftentimes, Aaron's platelet count would drop, so he needed blood transfusions. It was grueling.

One afternoon at the hospital, we ran into the famous hot dog man from Holmby Park. He was at Holmby Park every day with his car, and attached was a little trailer that held his grill. He sold hot dogs, french fries, and popsicles and had a very distinct rainbow-colored umbrella open above his car. When he didn't have any customers, he sat there under the umbrella watching the cars go by on Beverly Glen Boulevard.

Sometimes he kicked off his shoes and you could see his bright white socks from the other end of the block. Every day for years while we were building the house, I got my lunch from him at two-thirty or three in the afternoon. Now here he was in the same radiation treatment center as Aaron. It was very sad when he died.

It's hard to believe that through all of this, we never discussed anything that was happening. Aaron was from the same generation as my parents, and they didn't talk about these things. They just pushed up their shirtsleeves and got through it. This was a big difference between the two of us. I needed to talk about my feelings.

I had started seeing a therapist before Aaron was diagnosed. It was long overdue. I had a lot of feelings that had built up over the years, and I wanted to talk about them. There was no quiet desperation or anguish and there also wasn't a last straw. I was just finally ready to start talking. At the time, I didn't know that therapists had areas of specialization just like physicians.

The first therapist I saw was in Century City. She has since become the authority on getting men to "put a ring on it," as they say. I went two or three times but wasn't entirely comfortable. Turns out neither was she. At our last appointment she told me she couldn't help me. She said I had a lot of anger issues and referred me to a colleague who specialized in women and anger issues.

The second therapist was the right key. She worked out of home. Her office was in a space over her garage. It felt very private and personal. I did find, however, that I didn't care for the traditional fifty-minute hour. I was so introverted that by the time I finally got going, the fifty-minute hour was up. I adjusted my hour to ninety minutes. Initially I went once a week. Then it was twice a week and before I knew it I was going three times a week. I like to joke that the therapist couldn't shut me up.

I was so grateful to have the therapist as my support system during Aaron's treatment. It was a challenging time. I found I was reliving what I had gone through with my mother and I was confused by this, but the truth was, I was resentful of Aaron's illness.

It was such a relief when Aaron completed his radiation treatment and his scans came back clear. He had beaten the odds and triumphed over cancer a second time. I was happy to see my husband in good spirits as he recuperated from the torture he had endured.

Couples who are married as long as Aaron and I had been have a tendency to finish each other's sentences and intuitively read each other's minds. We were no exception to this. Shortly after his radiation treatment concluded, I noticed something was off but couldn't quite put my finger on it. One day I happened to overhear him in conversation with one of his assistants and it finally hit me.

"Stop answering for him. Let him answer for himself."

Aaron's assistant looked at me as if I had lost my mind. He was a clever man and a brilliant writer who knew how to cut in and out of dialogue. He had used the tricks of his trade to hide Aaron's memory loss. I asked Aaron to spell a word and he couldn't. Aaron Spelling, true to his name, was the world's best speller. When he couldn't spell a relatively simple word, the truth was undeniable. This also explained his resistance to seeing people and socializing.

By the time I caught on, it was late in the game. I needed to talk to someone who would know about Aaron's condition. Aaron and I had been close with former president Reagan and Nancy Reagan. Aaron and Ronnie had known each other since Aaron moved to Los Angeles in the mid-1950s. We had had them over quite a bit, so I felt comfortable sharing what was going on with Nancy. She of course had been through it herself with her husband while he was still in the White House, so I felt she was the right person to confide in.

Unfortunately for me, Nancy confirmed my fears. She urged me to take Aaron to see Dr. Jeffrey Cummings, chief of the Alzheimer's Unit at UCLA Medical Center. I promised Nancy I would make an appointment to see Dr. Cummings . . . and then I didn't. Aaron had always been a sharp mind, and now he seemed lost. I didn't know what to do with that. A few weeks later, I ran into Nancy, and she asked if we had been to see Dr. Cummings yet. Before I could say anything, Nancy was wagging her finger in my face. "I know you haven't made an appointment because I called Dr. Cummings and asked him."

I called and made the appointment the very next day. I very casually told Aaron that his regular doctor wanted him to see this "other doctor." I had to be very careful because the last time we had been to UCLA, it was a very negative experience for Aaron. I'm not sure exactly how I did it, but somehow I got Aaron into the car for the short ride to see Dr. Cummings.

I knew the doctor wasn't going to tell me anything about my husband's condition that I didn't already know. More than anything it was just a formality.

Aaron knew why we were there as soon as he read the sign for the Alzheimer's Unit. He looked at me with a very sad expression on his face. "I may have to kill you."

Once we were seated in Dr. Cummings's office, he asked Aaron who the president of the United States was, what day of the week it was, and what month we were in. They were all ridiculously simple questions, and Aaron couldn't answer any of them. I turned my head and cried. If I had any denial left in me, it was all gone now.

How could this happen to my brilliant husband? I was suddenly reminded that when I was pregnant, I never wanted to read all those books expectant mothers read. I figured whatever happens, happens. That was my approach to life. Aaron's cancer had made sense, but this was not a scenario I had ever imagined. Especially not for someone as imaginative and present as Aaron had been. The realization of what was happening to my husband took my breath away. I didn't want him to see me crying, but it was too late.

Alzheimer's is a brand name for dementia. We never found out 100 percent whether Aaron had Alzheimer's or dementia because he never followed through on the full battery of tests. It hardly mattered. They're different diseases but equally cruel and abusive to those afflicted.

I tried to keep things status quo throughout Aaron's illness. I made excuses for him when he didn't want to be seen by people and couldn't handle social situations. He was never particularly interested in going out when he was well, so this wasn't a good barometer of whether he knew his mind was failing him. In the beginning I wasn't certain whether he knew what was happening. Looking back now, I think on some level, he must have known.

I thought it might help to get him out of the house, but he wouldn't go and I couldn't force him. I continued going to dinner parties for Aaron's sake and mine. I went alone to places we would have gone as a couple. I made excuses for him and told people he wasn't feeling well because that's what Aaron wanted me to say. I don't know why, but I suddenly thought about all the times that Aaron would call the hostess of whichever party we were attending and insist we be seated together. Typically, couples sit apart so they can socialize, and I enjoyed sitting next to someone new and hearing about their life experiences. I was the shy one, but it was Aaron who didn't like sitting apart.

On this particular night, I realized I couldn't maintain the facade. I didn't want to lie anymore. It was towards the end when he really wasn't himself anymore that I needed a dose of reality. Maybe it wasn't fair of me, but I didn't want to live this way. It was such a feeling of relief to finally be truthful and say that Aaron didn't want to come to the party; that he couldn't come. I realized as soon as I finished the sentence that everyone knew the truth anyway. As relieved as I was, I also felt guilty as if I were betraying my husband.

Believe it or not, there were times when Aaron could still fake it. I would hear him on the phone with friends telling them that he had been at the office every day the week before. It broke my heart because he wanted so badly to believe he had been at the office. It reminded me of when he was still healthy and he told stories from when he was just nineteen years old and served in the Air Force during World War II. I never knew what was truth and what was fiction, but it didn't matter then because the stories were so entertaining.

I came home from the dinner party that night and told Aaron the truth. "I told everyone at the party you didn't want to go." He was mortified. "I can't keep covering for you." Tears welled up in my eyes. "Our friends keep looking at me like I have two heads."

After that, when we got invitations, I would RSVP for one. I went alone and nobody questioned me about Aaron anymore.

For most of my life, I had been Mrs. Aaron Spelling. For thirty-eight years his vision and creativity had defined our lives as a family. I thought about my own mother, how she had depended on my father her whole life and how angry she was. I was angry now too but in a different way. For my mother, on the surface at least, it was about money. When I married Aaron, she advised me to have what she called a "push-key" account of my own money in case the marriage didn't work out. This was never my fear with Aaron. We had built everything together. I had always believed in him. When he had his moments of frustration with partners, I told him he didn't need them and encouraged him to fulfill his dream of having his own production company. I had come a long way from sitting in the car while he met with the president of ABC-TV.

Weeks before we were married, Aaron's business manager had sent me a very aggressive prenuptial agreement. It was incredibly hurtful. Ironic too because at that time, I actually had more money than Aaron did. I had invested all of my money from the modeling I had done and created quite a little nest egg for myself. Aaron, on the other hand, had just started his own production company and in the divorce from Carolyn had signed away his half of the house they owned to avoid any acrimony. Aaron saw how ridiculous the prenuptial agreement was and literally tore it up right in front of me.

Over the course of thirty-eight years, I managed and invested all of our money. I don't think Aaron really ever knew how much money his shows had earned. I remember when the house next to ours in Malibu went up for sale and he wanted to buy it so that we could expand our existing house. Aaron asked me if we could afford it. I had to laugh. He was a generous spirit.

I was so naive. As I entered my fifties, I assumed we would be enjoying our first grandchild and maybe doing a little more traveling. I had raised my children, so now I saw myself busting loose a little, spending more time with my girlfriends. Instead, here I was at home watching the Alzheimer's quietly ravage my husband. It was so isolating. Many of our friends were already fading out of our lives. Our son, Randy, was doing the best he could to be there for his father, but it was proving to be too much for him.

Our daughter, Tori, had been incommunicado since getting an abrupt divorce from her husband, Charlie. Aaron had not been feeling well when we were planning her wedding, yet he mustered up the strength to walk his daughter down the aisle and be a gracious father of the bride at her wedding. The next morning he didn't have it in him to go up to the Bel-Air Hotel for the post-wedding brunch, so I went without him.

We actually hadn't heard from Tori since she left The Manor after her wedding reception. Aaron was disappointed about her divorce, and since then she had refused to speak to any of us on the phone. Not even her little brother.

My therapist understood the reasons behind my anger and assured me that it was quite common for spouses and caregivers to feel this way. She encouraged me to get out for a bit of self-preservation. She said it was like the oxygen masks on the airplane. I needed to take care of myself first so I could continue taking care of Aaron. Easier said than done.

Every time I went out to lunch with girlfriends, I would get six phone calls from Aaron asking when I would be home. I knew it was the Alzheimer's talking, but it was still tough. Sometimes I would just be arriving at the restaurant and he was already on the phone, "Are you through yet?"

I would try to explain, but he would grow agitated and unreasonable. "Are you on your way home?" There was nothing I could say or do. I wanted so badly to somehow revive his mind, make him remember who he was. Who we were.

One day I needed desperately to get out for a while, so I left Randy with Aaron. When I returned I was blindsided by the news that Tori and her new husband had stopped by to visit with Aaron. Tori and Randy had orchestrated a plan for Tori to stop by while I was out. It was hurtful but I understood Tori was in every way Randy's big sister, so he did as she requested. By this point, Aaron had suffered a stroke and was critically ill, so I'm not sure whether he was even aware that Tori was there.

A couple weeks later, I could see that the end was approaching quickly, so I started calling Aaron's friends, asking them to please come visit and say their goodbyes. Randy's friends had taken him on a much-needed guys' trip and they were flying back that day, so I texted him and I also texted one of his friends to call me as soon as they landed. We hadn't heard from Tori since she came by with her husband, so I sent her an e-mail hoping she would acknowledge it.

20

The End and the Beginning

While Aaron was bedridden, I learned to use a computer and surf the Internet. Shopping online for collectibles became my outlet. We had become accidental recluses. Staying at his side wasn't heroic, it was where I wanted to be and where so many other wives, husbands, and children remain when a loved one suffers the scourge of Alzheimer's. I felt grateful that we could keep Aaron at home and not have to rely on our health insurance to pay for an Alzheimer's unit at a hospital.

Somewhere I had read a disturbing statistic that a high percentage of spouses and caregivers suffer strokes and heart attacks from the stress of looking after a partner or family member with Alzheimer's. We had nurses and household help, but what I didn't have was another family member to shoulder the emotional responsibility. It was all on me, and it got harder every day.

This was my inspiration for getting away overnight every now and then to our house in Malibu. I would go there just to sleep. I would lay there at night on what I still called my side of the bed and look out the picture window in the master bedroom. I felt as if I were on a ship, sailing on the ocean.

The truth is, I've never been a beach person. Aaron loved the beach, and about forty years ago, we bought our house in Malibu. Aaron wanted it so badly, and even though we couldn't afford it, we bought it as Aaron's retreat. It was half the house then. Some years later, we bought the house next door to ours when it went on the market, and we combined the two of them.

I've never liked the feeling of sand under my feet, but Aaron, Tori, and Randy loved it. On my overnights in Malibu, I would sit outside on our deck remembering all of us walking on the shore together with our dogs. Everyone was in their bare feet, except for me. I always wore my tennis shoes. I remembered the sound of the crashing waves, the smell of the salt water, and the smiles.

Malibu has grown since we bought our first house there. I used to buy groceries at a small market nearby. Now there is a gourmet country market where you can buy the most delicious food. At the Malibu Country Mart, which is at the intersection of Pacific Coast Highway and Cross Creek, there are trattorias, sushi restaurants, and even a Greek restaurant where you can have a nice dinner out. There are upscale shops like James Perse and Ralph Lauren. The paparazzi hang out at the first pedestrian crosswalk at the Country Mart waiting for a famous face to show up, which they often do. While still rustic and peaceful there, it's just more glamorous.

There is the legend of wild parrots in Malibu. People say that years ago, one lone parrot escaped from his cage from one of the homes up on the hillside. Somehow one parrot became two and then they became four and so on. It's usually on Sunday afternoons that you can hear the wild parrots squawking. If you know where to look, you can see all the green parrots hiding up in the palm trees. Somehow they know it's Sunday and they come out to sing.

After Aaron died I spent more time in Malibu. More than I thought I would. The day following his death when his body was no longer in our home was the first day in almost thirty-nine years that I hadn't had to wake up and take care of him in some way. His funeral was very private and ended up just being family and close friends. I had originally planned to have a memorial service since Aaron was a public figure and there were fans of his shows all over the world. Then I thought, "Who would I invite?" "Would anyone want to come?" "Do I have the energy to plan a memorial?" I wasn't sure so I talked myself out of doing it.

It was after the funeral when my friend Willy went home after staying with me for three nights that I really felt Aaron's absence. I missed the sound of his voice and even the smell of his tobacco pipe. I also had to rehome his little white toy poodle, Precious, who had sat on the bed with him all day, every day for the two years that he was ill. Now that he was gone, she was fighting with my dog, Annie. Whenever I showed Annie any affection, Precious would get very feisty and attack her. I found Precious a home where she would be the lap dog of an elderly woman who was looking for a companion dog. Precious would go back to being the queen of the house the way she had been here. I knew she would be happier that way than at The Manor, which now seemed so empty.

There was something about the way I was feeling that surprised me. It wasn't the moments of suffocating grief or overwhelming confusion. It wasn't the loneliness. I expected all of those feelings. They rolled in like waves, and I learned to ride them up to their crest and then back down. What I hadn't expected was that I would feel absent.

It was seven or eight months after Aaron died that I moved out of Tori's bedroom and back into the master bedroom. My decorator and dear friend Robert Dally came out of retirement to help me. I couldn't be in the room the way it had been when Aaron was dying. For some reason, I also didn't want to be in there if it looked the way it had when it was "ours."

The room needed to be my own. We started by ordering new carpet and then new fabric. Once it looked entirely different, I moved back in.

Confirmation that I was truly on my own came via the United States Postal Service. It was an invitation, and for the first time ever, it wasn't addressed to Mr. and Mrs. Aaron Spelling or even to The Spellings. It was addressed to just me alone. I held it in my hand for a minute and absorbed the significance.

While Aaron had been ill, I had been out to numerous dinner parties without him. Because I was still the better half of Aaron Spelling, even when he wasn't with me, the conversation was focused on him. His whereabouts, his shows, his talents. I soon discovered that people have a tough time making conversation with you altogether after your husband dies. When he was sick, people asked how he was feeling. Now that he was gone and I was a widow, people were uncomfortable. They stared at me not knowing what to say.

I suppose in some ways I saw this day coming even before Aaron was sick. When we were first married, Aaron gave me some of his credit cards to use for household expenses and personal items. I made the assumption that he hadn't had time to add me as an additional user on the cards. They all said "Mrs. Aaron Spelling." It didn't take me long to figure out that this was how he saw me, and this was how he wanted it. Over the years when I approached the topic of getting a card in my own name, Aaron would say he didn't want to pay duplicate credit card fees. I knew this was just an excuse, but I also knew that I had married a very old-fashioned man, so I didn't push it.

Eventually I established credit in my own name. My first credit card was an American Express card. I loved seeing my name on the card. Instead of letting our business manager handle the statement, I made sure to pay it on time myself. I can't explain why it meant so much to me, but it did. I had been waiting for an opportunity to pick up the check at a restaurant. I remember the first time I did it with Aaron. He definitely didn't see it coming, and he sure didn't know what to think. Randy was also with us, and he was very surprised.

I understand it now. I wanted to feel that I was equal. In a strange way, it was like having the right to vote.

The thought of eating alone in a restaurant didn't bother me after Aaron had passed away. What I dreaded was the thought of a dinner party full of couples. Fortunately, the first dinner party I attended on my own was given by friends who had really stood by me in the thick of it. It was a rough evening, but it was the push I needed. After months of feeling disconnected and depressed, I woke up the next morning to the realization that I was still young and full of life. I missed my husband, but somehow I needed to figure out how to begin again.

I had no idea what this meant or how I was going to do it, but I knew I had to. I don't know why, but my mind wandered to the memories of being out with Aaron when every aspiring actor, writer, and producer came out of the woodwork. This happened at restaurants, bowling alleys, you name it. There was always someone who wanted to give Aaron a head shot or a script or pitch him a story. They always wanted to know the secret to his success. Aaron's answer was always the same: "*Follow Your Dreams.*"

Aaron often used the phrase "stardust" when he met a young actor or actress whom he thought had star quality. When he talked about people who would stand out in a crowd, he always said they had stardust in their eyes. I suddenly realized I needed to have stardust in my eyes. I needed to pick myself up and believe in myself. I wasn't sure what dreams the stardust would lead me to, but I told myself I should make sure I was seeing stardust and not just dust. They were two very different things.

Aaron Spelling as "Jerry Lane" on stage in 1944.

THE PLAYBILL

"WINE, WOMEN & SPAIN"
Starring Sgr. "Jerry Lane" Spelling

USO THEATRE   **PARIS, 1944**

The original Playbill of the 1944 USO
production of *Wine, Women & Spain*.

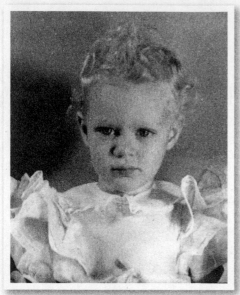

One of the first pictures of me, at 2–3 years old, that I was able to find in my collection.

As a child, here at 5 or 6 years old, I always loved my stuffed animals.

The happiest day of my life, becoming Mrs. Aaron Spelling on November 23, 1968.

Here with my mother, Gene, and my father, Merritt, as
two families became one on November 23, 1968.

A gathering of friends and immense talent with Ginny Newhart, Aaron, me, Mark
Nathanson, Dean Martin, Catherine Martin, Dick Martin, and Bob Newhart.

Always full of humorous stories, Aaron telling another with
Nolan Miller and Barbara Stanwyck around 1971.

Entertaining the night away with guests like Army Archerd in 1971.

Reminiscing about *The Mod Squad* days, with Clarence Williams III, Tige Andrews, Peggy Lipton, and Michael Cole in 1971.

Never a dull moment hosting the likes of Esther Williams, Marlo Thomas, and Anne Francis in 1971.

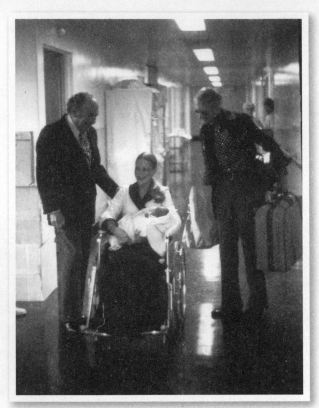

In 1973, Aaron and I left the hospital with our daughter, Tori— an unforgettable day!

Aaron was always the charmer, engaging the beautiful Natalie Wood and Robert Wagner at a party in 1977 at our house.

1979, Aaron and I photographed for the Life & Style section of *LA Times*.

I was so proud to have Aaron at the opening of Lehr & Spelling, here with ABC Entertainment vice president Gary Pudney and president Tony Thomopoulos.

APPETIZING BOUTIQUE — ABC Entertainment vice president Gary Pudney, far left, and president Tony Thomopoulos, far right, join Aaron and Candy Spelling at opening of Candy Spelling and Marcia Lehr's boutique on Canon Drive. Lehr-Spelling Boutique specializes in party planning and special gifts with a candy store full of confectionary delights.

New Year's Eve celebrations were always spectacular; in 1982 we celebrated with many friends, including Ricardo and Georgiana Montalbán and Hervé Villechaize.

The festivities were always so exciting to see all the glamour, here with Georgiana and Ricardo Montalbán in 1982.

There was never a shortage of creativity at our parties; Lee Majors and Dionne Warwick were just a couple of the amazingly gifted guests at our New Year's Eve party in 1982.

I can remember this evening like it was yesterday, here with John Forsythe and wife Julie.

Moments before the clock struck 12 in 1982, Teri Garr and Michael Keaton.

Bringing in 1983, Joan Collins, Dionne Warwick, Shirley
Jones, and Lee Majors, such a fantastic group of people.

We always had a superb mix of people; we celebrated frequently with both entertainment
friends and political friends. Mayor Tom Bradley joined us in ringing in 1983.

Berry Gordy always brought that extra amount of fun to the party.

Aaron always worked the room, giving everyone a bit of him, here with Hervé Villechaize at our New Year's Eve party in 1982.

Eva Gabor and Lloyd Bridges danced the new year in;
I loved watching everyone enjoying themselves.

Robyn and Fred Astaire left me awestruck.

I think I would have fainted if Fred Astaire had asked me to dance that New Year.

*Lehr and Spelling announces with glee
That it's their first Anniversary.
It's been a year since the fun began.
So Marcia and Candy have a plan.
To celebrate their success (and it's been
that—and more—)
They're having a week-long party at
their store.
From August 1st through the 6th, with
great pleasure and pride,
They'll "thank you" for being right there
at their side.
Refreshments will flow—bring this
card in—here's why—
They'll give you a gift to remember
them by.*

*Lehr and Spelling
345 North Canon Drive
Beverly Hills, California 90210*

Telephone (213) 278-8200

The official invitation for
the first anniversary of
Lehr & Spelling in 1983.

The first anniversary of Lehr & Spelling was such an incredible celebration here with Aaron, Marcia Lehr, and me with Governor Brown in 1983.

Governor Brown was so gracious in stopping in for the first-year anniversary, here with Marcia Lehr and me in 1983.

She is the epitome of class, and I am so honored to call her my friend, with Nancy Reagan at Lew Wasserman's birthday.

To Candy Spelling
With best wishes,
Nancy Reagan

A day at the races with Suzanne Pleshette in 1984.

One of my favorite photos of Tori and Randy.

At a party for *The Love Boat*, John Forsythe was always such a gentleman.

In 1986 with the country superstar Kenny Rogers and his then-wife Marianne Rogers.

One of my favorite couples, Anne and Kirk Douglas, in 1987.

Charlton Heston with wife, Lydia, were always a pleasure to host, here in 1987.

John Forsythe with then-wife Julie exemplified true Hollywood glamour.

Entertaining with *Hotel* co-stars James Brolin and Connie Sellecca in 1987.

One of my favorite party guests, my handsome son, Randy.

So many legends in one place: Georgiana Montalbán, Kirk Douglas, Altovise Davis, Sammy Davis Jr., and Ricardo Montalbán in 1987.

Sammy Davis Jr. was always a treat, with Linda Evans, Richard Cohen, Sandra Moss, and Altovise Davis in 1987.

Aaron and I always reveled in the intimate moments alone at the various parties and social events.

The talented Lionel Richie and then-wife Brenda Richie never failed to bring flair to the party, here in 1987.

The Spelling family looking very Dynasty in this photo.

In 1988, it was such a pleasure to spend the evening with my own personal icon in Aaron and another legend, Jimmy Stewart and his wife Gloria.

In the early 90s, Tori was asked to host a grad night at Universal Studios in Orlando, Florida. What a great memory!

Aaron and I always enjoyed the holidays, especially Christmas as here in 1991. There was never a shortage of festive decorations and beautifully wrapped presents.

Aaron was famous for attracting some of the most intriguing people into a conversation, here in 1992 with Merv Griffin and Jack Carter.

One of our dearest friends, Joel Schumacher, helped us celebrate our 25th wedding anniversary.

In 1992, one of Aaron's favorite pianists, Michael Feinstein, performed for our 25th anniversary.

Carole Bayer Sager and Joel Schumacher at our 25th wedding anniversary.

Cutting the cake 25 years later proved to be just as romantic as it was in 1968 on our wedding day.

Such a phenomenal gift having Michael Feinstein perform at our 25th wedding anniversary.

I always loved visiting Aaron at his office; he was a creative genius! Here in 1993.

Gathering with our guests like Angela Lansbury and Peter Shaw in 1994, waiting for Prince Charles to arrive at The Manor.

One of the most memorable events Aaron and I hosted at The Manor in 1994. It was wonderful seeing all of our dearest friends meeting HRH Prince Charles. From left to right, Governor Wilson and his wife, Aaron and I, and Lew and Edie Wasserman.

I was so nervous sitting beside Prince Charles for the evening.

Centro de Niños has always been near and dear to both my heart and my family's.
Angie and Richard Alatorre, Randy, Tori, and Aaron and I with
Sandy Serrano-Sewell in 1995.

Combining my love of dolls with one of my favorite organizations, Centro de Niños, I am always looking for ways to empower children.

I love hosting my friends, especially for their remarkable milestones. Here is Suzanne Pleshette, Johnny Carson, and Jack Valenti celebrating Edie Wasserman's 80th birthday in 1993.

The Manor was filled frequently with gentlemen toasting to their friendships and business endeavors, something Johnny Carson, Steve Lawrence, and Aaron were famous for.

Another great night filled with friends like Eydie and Steve Lawrence with Edie Wasserman.

Normally very private, Aaron connecting with his loyal fans at his book signing in 1996 was wonderful to see. Here a fan presented Aaron with a poster from his first acting job from 1954.

I was so proud of Aaron for all of his accomplishments; it was thrilling to see how well received his autobiography was. The fans adored him in 1996.

In 1996, Aaron and I were honored with the Fulfillment Award from the Fulfillment Fund at UCLA, a nonprofit organization helping Los Angeles students overcome obstacles to achieve a college education.

Jaclyn Smith, a good friend, came to support us at the Fulfillment Award ceremony in 1996.

Legendary NBA star Shaquille O'Neal inspires many of the students benefiting from the Fulfillment Fund organization.

Setting the perfect table during the holidays is tedious but one of my favorite things. This is Thanksgiving 1996.

One of Aaron's favorite talents, Joan Collins, here at Christmastime at The Manor.

At Christmas in 1998, Aaron left me awestruck with the most gorgeous set of diamonds and black onyx. The necklace, bracelet, ring, and earrings left me speechless.

Some of the best times have been spent traveling with close friends, especially one of my dearest, Ghada Irani, here with Andrea Bocelli.

In 2000, Aaron and I opened The Manor for the first annual Centro de Niños Easter Egg Hunt. It was unforgettable watching all of the children race to the eggs.

Lifelong friends were always important to Aaron, here with Red Buttons in 2002.

Aaron always gave time for charity; here at an event with philanthropic Barbara Davis in 2002 at The Manor.

Aaron never failed to have a good time at celebrations, even with prolific talents like Sumner Redstone and Diahann Carroll.

In 2003, Tony Danza, Aaron, and I.

A night full of stars, here in 2003 with the likes of Barbara Davis, John Travolta, Kelly Preston, Don Rickles, Sidney Poitier, and Ghada and Ray Irani.

A special Christmas celebrated in 2004 with Joanna and Sidney Poitier.

Joel Schumacher in 2004 was a customary guest during the holidays.

It was one of my greatest pleasures serving as a commissioner for the Department of Recreation and Parks, here with Los Angeles mayor Antonio Villaraigosa around 2004.

One of my loves, cooking in the kitchen and sharing fabulous recipes, in 2008.

The dining room has always been one of my favorite rooms—
it is where we gather with our friends and family to catch up.

Enjoying a Christmas holiday at Griffith Park with LA's BEST.

It is a treat to go to class with some of the children
benefiting from one of my favorite charities, LA's BEST.

Leaving the classroom and marching
outside with the children from LA's BEST.

21

Stardust

I proceeded with cautious optimism. I wasn't entirely confident about venturing out into the real world, so I thought that exploring the world via the Internet was the safest way to go. Before I could do this, I needed to learn how to do more than shop on the Internet, so I hired a computer tutor. He taught me how to open multiple browser windows and Google people, places, and things, as well as send attachments like jpegs. Soon I was reading online news sources and posts by bloggers. I felt like Magellan as I navigated my way around the new world of the virtual globe.

Then there were times I would click through to a site or try to upload a file or download one, and I wasn't sure how I had gotten to that point. I tried to retrace my steps, but it was digital overload. It felt like I was in high school trying to pass the Beverly Hills High School "Senior Problems" examination all over again.

Despite my frustrations I was not deterred. I felt more secure exploring the possibilities that might be out there for me in the privacy of my home. I know I'm really dating myself here, but I had a great deal of affection for "letting your fingers do the walking" in the Yellow Pages.

Over the years we hired many vendors for the house and for our parties, not to mention dog groomers, straight out of the Yellow Pages. People were always so surprised that we did that. Sometimes it worked out and sometimes it didn't, but it was what we did back then. We also used the big fat book as a booster seat at restaurants when they didn't have any. And back in my modeling days, we used the slimmer version of the Yellow Pages balanced on our heads to practice walking with perfect posture.

I was resistant to letting go of my phone book until one day when I wanted to look up a former neighbor to see how she was doing. It was nothing short of magical that I could Google her and contact her through one of the social media sites. I sure couldn't do that with the Yellow Pages. One day I discovered the Yellow Pages was available online, complete with customer reviews. I knew then I needed to build my own Candy Spelling website and step out of the shadows.

I hired a friend of a friend to build me a cute and user-friendly website. As soon as it was live, I started getting e-mails on a daily basis. I got fan mail and hate mail, e-mails from fans of Aaron's shows, and one day, an e-mail from Bravo's Andy Cohen. Soon after came a message from an executive at Disney. They both wanted to kick around ideas for television shows. Honestly, I had to pinch myself.

In the meantime, my friend's husband who was an agent had agreed to represent me. His name was David Shapira, and he must have had a book in mind because one day he showed up with Elizabeth Beier, a senior editor from St. Martin's Press. He was a smart man and kept whatever he was thinking to himself. There was no spotlight on me, so I was completely comfortable chatting with the editor in what seemed like just a social setting. I was clueless and had absolutely no idea I was actually in a pitch meeting.

I started telling her the now-infamous Rock Hudson bathroom story and she stopped me cold.

"Can you write that down as a treatment?"

I did as she asked, and two weeks later I had a book deal. Honestly, nobody was more shocked than I was. It was incredibly exciting and scary all at the same time. The book was my story. My life before I met Aaron, our courtship, and also my life as a wife and mother against the backdrop of Hollywood. I thought it would be fun to share a glimpse into that time that was our own legendary Camelot.

The approach to the book was very creative and whimsical. It was a scrapbook template of sorts that was perfect for me because I am an avid scrapbook enthusiast and collector of memories. When I delivered the book to St. Martin's, I had it gift wrapped (of course!) and placed in an original *90210* messenger bag.

The book tour was like my coming-out party. It was big adventure and reminded me a bit of taking the Cannonball across the country. This time around I was going to fly, and I wouldn't have fifty pieces of luggage in tow.

We kicked off the book tour at Borders Books in New York City (it's a Barnes & Noble now) at the Time Warner Center. We also went out to Long Island and then on to Chicago. In Seattle, it was pouring rain, and I slipped and fell before the book signing. Fortunately I didn't get hurt and had a change of clothes with me. In Dallas, a wonderful book club threw a luncheon for me. In Houston, philanthropist Lynn Wyatt threw a lovely party for me. Then it was back home to California, where I made appearances at Book Soup, Vromann's in Pasadena, and Barnes & Noble at The Grove.

Initially I was a bit panicked because this would be my first time speaking in public. I didn't want to read excerpts out loud because of my eye convergence insufficiency. I was also hesitant to read from a teleprompter because I thought it would seem too forced. The thought of losing my place on the teleprompter seemed to have potentially disastrous consequences.

Instead of using written words on a teleprompter, I decided to have visual aids on a screen so I could refer to them while I was speaking. It was the most comfortable option for me, sort of like having someone hold your hand. Well, Murphy's Law caught up to me pretty quickly, and at my very next appearance in Huntington, New York, at a store called Book Revue. Technical difficulties prevented my visual aids from going up, and unlike television in which you can cut to the color bars, I was live, so I had to wing it.

This minor disaster turned out to be the best thing that could have happened for my book tour, not to mention the best possible thing for my self-confidence. Interacting with the audience turned out to be much more fun than reading from a script, and I wound up staying for an hour longer than I was supposed to. I didn't feel like I was on stage at all. It was like chatting with friends in my own yard at one of our barbecues.

My book tour gave me a new appreciation for anyone who goes on a promotional tour for a movie, television show, or a cause they believe in. As much as I was enjoying it, traveling to a new city every couple of days was not easy. I was amazed that people stood in line for so long to see me or hear me speak. I happily chatted and signed books for everyone who was kind enough to show up for me.

Promoting the book challenged me in so many ways. I was really nervous about doing television, but I knew I had to do it. The more I did it, the more I just forgot the camera was there and that anybody was watching. In the end, I did nine television shows and three radio shows.

My appearance on *The View* was definitely the unexpected low point of my promotional tour. It's a bit of a blur now, but I distinctly remember being ripped apart by hosts Elisabeth Hasselbeck and Joy Behar. It didn't matter that neither one of them had any facts; they had already found me guilty. It was so awful. Barbara Walters and Whoopi Goldberg tried their best to intervene, but it was too late, I had already been thrown to the lions.

I left the studio in tears. Whoopi was very sweet and followed me to the door and put her arms around me. I think because Whoopi is a mother and a grandmother, she understood the complexities I was dealing with. Barbara is of course a veteran journalist, and despite her intimidating persona, she refrained from judging me. She has her own daughter, so I think she approached me with a more balanced perspective.

It was definitely the school of hard knocks, but I had signed up for it. I had no choice but to dust myself off and get back on the horse. Which is exactly what I did.

Stories from Candyland was ultimately a huge success story and ended up on *The New York Times* Best-Seller List. It was a much needed boost to my morale. It also gave me a huge sense of accomplishment to add the title of "author" to my resume.

The stars must have been aligned because shortly after the book, producer Ryan Seacrest approached me about appearing on a game show he was producing for E!. The show was called *Bank of Hollywood* and was an adaptation of the British television show called *Fortune: Million Pound Giveaway*. The premise of *Bank of Hollywood* was for contestants to come on the show and pitch their ideas to a celebrity panel of judges known as the "power panel." I had to pinch myself again that Ryan Seacrest wanted me as a judge. I was very flattered by what Ryan said about me in an interview with the *Los Angeles Times*: "'One of the key components to this show' is sniffing out the phony requests. . . . 'She was in charge of a lot of Aaron's empire off the television shows, so she can really see through people and read agendas.'"

Our panel included me; Sean Patterson, the president of Wilhelmina Models; Melody Thornton of *The Pussycat Dolls;* and Vanessa Rousso, a world-class professional poker player who was the top-earning woman on the professional poker tour. The hopeful contestants would plead their cases, and we would take it to a vote. If majority ruled, the contestants were awarded the prize money.

Bank of Hollywood reminded me quite a bit of the show *Queen for a Day,* which was on the air when I was a teenager. It had actually started as a radio show when I was probably just learning to walk. It was on in the middle of the day, five days a week. It became so popular with women that NBC made it a prime-time show. Jack Bailey, a former vaudeville performer, was the host, and at the beginning of every episode he would bellow, "Do YOU want to be queen for a day?" The audience would go wild with applause. The show was entertaining but sad when it came right down to it. The contestants would tell their heartwrenching stories in an attempt for the big giveaway at the end of the show. In this case, it was the Applause-meter that determined who would be crowned Queen for the day.

Instead of money, *Queen for a Day* always gave away a refrigerator or a washer and dryer "furnished by" the program's advertising sponsor. The winner had a crown placed on her head and was also given a faux sable robe along with a bouquet of roses. Jack Bailey ended every show by saying, "Make every woman queen for every single day." If you think about it, *Queen for a Day* was one of the first reality shows. What we all found out later was that those poor women had the crown, robe, and roses taken away immediately after the show ended. They also had to find someone to buy whatever they had won because they had to pay the taxes on it.

Some of the contestants on *Bank of Hollywood* were very inspiring. There was an urban dance troupe who came on the show. The founder of the troupe was asking for $31,000 for dance scholarships. They gave an impressive performance when they came out, and the founder's plea was very emotional. Sean Patterson had to ask one of the other members of the troupe to speak on behalf of the group. Through her we learned that the troupe really was more of a family and support group that helped the members set and achieve goals.

There was also a very charming aspiring actor, Tedrick, who wanted funding for acting classes. Sean Patterson really put him through the paces and made him improvise interviewing Melody on a red carpet. Tedrick actually did a terrific job. I thought he had serious potential. It was a 3-to-1 vote in his favor. There were also some less altruistic contestants and others that bordered on the ridiculous. One young woman came on the show to plead her case for a right-hand driving car. We were in Los Angeles, for crying out loud. In her case we voted unanimously not to fund her.

Even with the sillier requests, I still felt a huge responsibility to the contestants. I mean, here they were in front of us and on national television pitching their hearts out. All in all it was a fun opportunity for me, and as the *Bank of Hollywood,* we were able to have a positive impact on the daily lives of some of our contestants.

I never expected I would form such a bond with the other judges. We all had such distinct backgrounds. The show was broadcast about the same time that *Keeping Up with the Kardashians* was just hitting the airwaves. The Kardashian show was proving to be very popular, so the time slot for *Bank of Hollywood* got moved around a few times and ultimately didn't do well. When we wrapped production, I invited everyone over to The Manor. It was well after midnight, so I called my security personnel ahead of time and told him I was bringing home a bunch of friends. This was new for me, and I could tell he was shocked.

"You're kidding, right?"

Whoever said "youth is wasted on the young" was 100 percent right. We ended up having a late-night party. It was good to be young again.

22

Business Is Business

Aaron was always full of good ideas, and he also enjoyed investing in talented people. In some cases it was writers on his shows or shows he was trying to sell to the network. He would come up with the idea, say, for example, a man on an island who grants wishes. He would write all of the broad strokes and then hand it over to a writer to draft the teleplay. I honestly couldn't believe he was willing to pay annuities to a writer for writing a script he was going to have to do a polish on later. He always had the same response.

"I get better writers this way."

Aaron wasn't only interested in seeing writers succeed. He really had an eye for talented people. I had a friend, Marcia Lehr, who was am amazing calligrapher and party planner. In the mid-1970s, she started her little side business by addressing envelopes for five cents each. By the time I met her, she was the best calligrapher and party planner in town. She had done quite a few of our parties, and it was obvious she was a true artist with a special gift.

Ever the producer with his eye out for talent, Aaron saw an opportunity to help Marcia shine by being an angel investor in a retail storefront. I knew from working at Jax that running a store was a lot of work. I could only imagine that opening a store would have been completely overwhelming for one person. Even though I had never managed a store, I had retail experience and good instincts. Combined with Marcia's brilliance, I knew we'd be a winning team, and so Lehr & Spelling was born.

As usual, Aaron wasn't entirely on board with my having responsibilities outside the home, but we worked it out. The idea was to have a one-stop gift shop with items ranging from candy to antique silverware. It took us just over a year to get the store up and running. The time we spent doing the buying alone was considerable. I always laugh when I think of all the time we spent just tasting the chocolate we were going to sell. I don't have a very big sweet tooth anyway, but after months of tasting chocolate, I finally started bringing it home and having the family taste it.

We rented space on Canon Drive in Beverly Hills. It was the perfect location because it put us right there in the middle of the famed Beverly Hills shopping district. I focused on buying the fixtures for the store and designing the space. Strangely enough, I went with a very modern look for the store. It was a very clean design with lots of chrome and a black granite candy counter. I don't know where this inspiration came from because my homes have always been decorated very traditionally.

I also went to stores like Tiffany and Cartier that offered corporate discounts. I got their applications for corporate accounts so I could use them as a template. I took what I liked best from all of those applications and made our own form. We quickly established corporate accounts for ABC, NBC, and Sunday Give Away at Hollywood Park, just to name a few.

Unfortunately, it was also my job to deal with the Health Department. They gave me a lot of trouble as I quickly became acquainted with their regulations. Honestly, some of the rules just made no sense. One that stands out in my mind required us to have a commercial-grade dishwasher in the back because we were selling candy containers. When it came to the gift wrapping, I was the one who was particular. When I interviewed gift wrappers, I had them wrap an empty box so that I could see their technique.

Getting all of the merchandise on the shelves was an unbelievable amount of work. Our inventory included stationary, Lucite frames, chocolate, toys, and all kinds of trinkets for kids. I even put in an engraving machine. Finally we were ready to open our doors.

After a weeklong grand opening that put us on the map, *People* magazine touted, "Candy, too, has proved she's no slouch at turning a profit. . . . Despite shaky economic times, the shop, Lehr & Spelling, is already thriving." It was true. Lehr & Spelling had taken on a life of its own. I was working in the store during the day and running back and forth between the store and The Manor, which was still under construction. Sometimes I was at the store until two or three in the morning because I had decided to personally wrap all the packages that needed wrapping. We didn't have the space for a customer service area where we could wrap the gifts, so I could only wrap at night when the store was closed.

Retail was hard for Marcia. It was definitely different from the very social job of party planning. I remember it well from my days at Jax. Customers are not your best friends. The success of the store was also hard on Aaron, who wanted me home for him. Between The Manor, the store, and being a mother, there wasn't a lot of time left for my husband. Aaron told me I needed to learn to delegate, but I knew the real solution was to give up working at the store.

Two years later, Lehr & Spelling closed its doors, but it was still a happy ending. Marcia's little family stationery business went on to become the go-to designer for celebrity invitations and announcements. For the last twenty five years or so her son, Sol Lehr, and her daughter, Ellen Black, have been creating stationery for the biggest names in Hollywood.

Business is business and I had succeeded in the enterprises I had tried on my own: QVC and Lehr & Spelling. My profits and proceeds from my doll collection were donated to Centro de Niños, and I never took a salary at the gift shop. I didn't take either one on for the money. I did it because there is something about working and earning money that creates a sense of self-worth and independence that can't be measured in dollars and cents.

With Aaron gone now, I could hop on a plane and go anywhere. I had plenty of time on my hands, but that wasn't where my heart was. I wanted to try my hand at another business, but I didn't have one in mind because I hadn't done enough to know what my niche was yet. I put out my feelers in Hollywood and hoped they would travel across the country to New York, "jump over the pond," and find their way to London before returning back here to me in Los Angeles.

I knew people were wondering why I wanted to get paid. My stock answer was that it was a way to validate my self-esteem. What I really wanted to say was that earning a paycheck was very different from making an investment with money left over from an allowance given to me by my husband.

23

Break a Leg

ven though *Bank of Hollywood* was canceled, my appearance on the show made an impression on producers Craig Zadan and Neil Meron. They were the producing team behind the film musicals *Hairspray* and *Chicago*. Now they were doing a television show called *Drop Dead Diva* for the Lifetime Network. The premise is that a gorgeous and vapid aspiring model named Deb dies in a fatal car accident. Deb finds herself at the gates of heaven and pleads with the gatekeeper to return her to her former fabulous existence. After declaring her a "self-centered zero," the gatekeeper relegates Deb to the body of a recently deceased plus-size attorney named Jane. The ongoing theme of the show is Deb trying to reconcile beauty with brains.

Drop Dead Diva is a very cute and life-affirming show with a powerful message for women. The list of guest stars is incredible: Paula Abdul, Delta Burke, Elliott Gould, Cybill Shepherd, Valerie Harper, and Liza Minnelli are just the ones I've managed to catch on the show. I was unbelievably flattered when Craig and Neil offered me a guest role on the show. I thought about it, but the honest truth is that there was absolutely no way I could memorize all the lines and be natural on camera. I did well on *Bank of Hollywood*, especially for someone who is fundamentally shy. Quite a few performers have stage fright, so it wasn't just the stage fright that kept me off of *Drop Dead Diva* because I am unequivocally just not an actress.

I knew that Craig and Neil had a company called Storyline Entertainment and had been nominated something like eight times for Emmy Awards and that *Chicago* had won six Oscars including Best Picture. By the way, that was the first time a musical had been awarded Best Picture since 1968, when *Oliver* won.

Still, I stuck with my gut and didn't sign on for the part on *Drop Dead Diva*. Even though I wasn't going to be their next guest star, I developed a friendship with Craig and Neil. At the time, they were producing their first Broadway venture and asked me to join them as a producer for the remake of the Broadway musical *Promises, Promises*.

The more I thought about making my first foray into the New York theater scene with visionary producers like Craig and Neil showing me the way, the more it felt like it was meant to be. Another reason I felt like it was the perfect fit for me was because it wasn't film or television, and I wouldn't be standing on the shoulders of my late husband. I think one of the reasons Aaron didn't dabble in the world of Broadway was because it would have meant numerous trips to New York, and it just wouldn't have worked traveling by train all the time.

I always like to do research before I get involved with a project. So before I started work on *Promises, Promises*, I watched the film *The Apartment*, which is what the play is based on. *The Apartment* is considered one of the greatest movies of all time. It's a romantic drama that was released in 1960 and stars Jack Lemmon, Shirley MacLaine, and Fred MacMurray. It was directed by Billy Wilder, who also directed *Some Like It Hot*. *The Apartment* was a huge commercial success and was also well received by critics. *New York Times* critic Bosley Crowther called it "a gleeful, tender and even sentimental film." The movie was honored with six Academy Awards.

In 1968, *The Apartment* became the basis for the original Broadway production of *Promises, Promises*. It starred Jerry Orbach, whom most of us know from *Law and Order,* and the lovely Jill O'Hara, who played the roommate Sheila in the original off-Broadway production of *Hair*. She went on to be nominated for a Tony Award for her performance in the original production of *Promises, Promises*. Burt Bacharach did the music, Hal David wrote the lyrics, and Neil Simon did the book. It was this production that gave birth to the classic songs "I'll Never Fall in Love Again" and "I Say A Little Prayer." The London production followed soon thereafter and opened in 1969 starring Tony Roberts and Betty Buckley.

Once I was officially a part of the producing team, I flew to New York City for the rehearsals. I was so nervous. As I walked into the theater, I felt like it was my first day of school. I honestly didn't know if I was allowed to talk to anyone. I was in awe when the marquee went up and there was my name in lights. I had goose bumps the whole time I stood there taking pictures of it. It was stardust, after all, and not just dust.

On the opening night of the previews, Neil Simon was sitting right behind me. I'll never forget when he said, "Candy, you will never experience this again. The audience was so in tune with the show."

I had worked with Aaron so much behind the scenes on the interior design and costuming of his shows. He always gave me credit, but I still felt invisible. Here was my chance to step up be recognized, and it meant even more because it was a revival of a musical on Broadway and not a revival of a show my husband had created.

Craig and Neil had updated the play so that it would be more modern. It was energetic and funny. The show went into previews at the end of March and opened on April 25, 2010. There was a lot of buzz about Katie Finneran's portrayal of Marge. She was dubbed a "scene stealer" by *The Wall Street Journal,* and less than two months into the show, they predicted she would win a Tony Award—and she did just that.

When *Promises, Promises* took its final bow in January 2011 after 1,281 performances, I was ready for my next challenge, which happened to be another show with Craig and Neil. This time it was the 50th Anniversary of *How to Succeed in Business Without Really Trying*. Actor Daniel Radcliffe, better known as Harry Potter, was taking on the lead role in the show as the New York City window cleaner, J. Pierrepont Finch.

The original stage production of *How to Succeed in Business Without Really Trying* was an adaptation of the 1952 book by Shepherd Mead. The book was a satire of corporate America and became a bestseller. With the popularity of the book there was an early attempt to adapt it into a play, but it wasn't successful, and the adaptation just languished. Years later, the creative team from *Guys and Dolls* became involved, and they retooled the adaptation to include a romance in the story. I think the love story combined with the songs of Frank Loesser must have clinched it because the show went into previews in August 1961.

Robert Morse from *Mad Men* played J. Pierrepont Finch in the original 1961 Broadway production, which also featured Charles Nelson Reilly in the role of Bud Frump. The musical was remounted in 1995 with Matthew Broderick playing Finch. In our 50th-Anniversary revival, *The New York Times* called Daniel Radcliffe "The Wizard of Corporate Climbing."

I must have flown to New York City eighteen times that year and stayed for three-week stretches. It didn't feel like work to me. It was a joy to be in the theater watching the rehearsals. The emotional return on my investment was already coming back to me tenfold. It was wonderful being away from Los Angeles. The hustle and bustle of Manhattan was the best vitamin injection anyone could ask for. Walking the red carpet at the Tony Awards was also very special for me because it was the first time I was photographed as myself and identified as a producer of a show. I was no longer just Aaron Spelling's wife or Tori Spelling's maleficent mother.

Over the years I had learned it takes hundreds of crew members to create a show or a production. Even producers have their respective areas of expertise. Some are great at working with writers while others handle heavy-duty decision-making. Craig and Neil and I were all on the same page when it came to my role as co-producer. We all felt handling the merchandising for the show would be my strong suit. I was extremely confident in my knowledge of merchandising. Going all the way back to *The Mod Squad*, Aaron's shows spurred lunch boxes, gum, trading cards, and of course T-shirts and posters. By the time Aaron was making *90210* and its spin-off, *Melrose Place*, his production company had a partnership with a merchandising company called Worldvision.

What always started out as Aaron asking my opinion about merchandise for a specific show ended up with me assuming responsibility for creating the merchandise. *90210* presented us with a whole variety of youth market options including nail polish, backpacks, jewelry boxes, messenger bags, and of course T-shirts, sweatshirts, and baseball caps. We also made a line of dolls based on the characters with Mattel. *Melrose Place* had many of the same items, but because the cast was a group of twentysomethings who hung out at *Shooters,* we also made souvenir shot glasses and T-shirts from the fictitious bar.

My cumulative experience at Jax, Lehr & Spelling, QVC, and of course all of Aaron's shows gave me an exceptional base of knowledge.

I started by sending inquiries to probably a dozen merchandising companies. Some of them specialized in Broadway shows and others handled concerts and live events but were willing to accommodate our needs. The bids came in, and it turned out to be better to go with a vendor who specialized in Broadway shows. At the end of the day, we produced T-shirts and hats fashioned to fit the style of the show. And of course we had to have the signature bow tie worn by J. Pierrepont Finch. We also had books, scores, and CDs, all of which sold in the kiosk at the theater.

I was very proud of our merchandising sales. The theatergoers went mad for the merchandise. As reported by *Playbill*, we had record-breaking ticket sales the week of Daniel's final performance.

That week may have been the last for Daniel, but it was just the beginning for me. I had found the niche I was looking for. When another company offered me the opportunity to be involved with *Nice Work If You Can Get It*, I was thrilled to jump on board. This show was described to me as "Gershwin, girls, and glamour." They had me at Gershwin. The show, which takes its name from the Gershwin song, is set in the 1920s Prohibition era. It is filled with the most captivating music and dance numbers. Matthew Broderick, who played the lead role of Jimmy Winter, was just fabulous, and the director Kathleen Marshall honestly just astounded me with her talent.

The show just had its final performance in June 2013. It was nominated for and won several Tony Awards as well as Drama Desk Awards and Drama League Awards. It was nice work for someone who just a couple of years ago was doing some serious soul searching, and now everything was falling into place.

Last year, I had remarkably good fortune once again when I was introduced to Scott Sanders, an Emmy– and Tony Award–winning theater, film, and television producer whose earlier shows included *The Color Purple* and *Evita*. He was well on his way to putting together another musical with a brilliant creative team that included Warren Carlyle, Daryl Waters, Isabel Toledo, and Wynton Marsalis's the Jazz at Lincoln Center All-Stars. He asked me to join as a producer, and it was thrilling to be there for the first preview and see the crowd up on their feet dancing and swaying to the big-band songs of Duke Ellington. Even more exciting was opening night and the rave reviews that followed proclaiming *After Midnight* a "must-see" for all.

24

Sex and the City of Angels

Somewhere between my writing the book, producing plays on Broadway, and selling The Manor, my girlfriends decided that I needed to start dating. They reminded me that it was one thing to have found my career-woman self, but now I needed to get back to dating so I could have balance.

Saying that my core group of girlfriends urged me to date is an understatement. Forced me is more like it, really. Now in order for me to talk about dating, I need to change the names of the innocent. Just like in *Dragnet*, "Ladies and Gentlemen, the story you are about to hear is true. Only the names have been changed to protect the innocent." In this case the names have been changed to protect the guilty as well.

After Aaron died I wasn't ready to date or even think about dating for quite awhile. To be honest, it was the furthest thing from my mind. After about a year, my friends kept saying that I needed to get out there and do whatever. It was the "whatever" part that made it all so difficult for me. It was daunting to think about. I hadn't done any dating since I was nineteen years old and started dating

Aaron. Except for one or two dates during our breakups before we were married, Aaron was it. How was it possible that I was going to start dating again and at my age? From what I could tell, "dating" had an entirely different connotation than it had more than three decades ago. In my day, a date was dinner and a movie, or if you were feeling ambitious, dinner, a movie, and dancing.

As I mulled it over, I could hear the trumpets from *The Dating Game* television show with Jim Lange. I tried to picture myself on that high stool, asking questions of three eligible bachelors on the other side of the partition.

The bottom line when it came to the topic of dating was the fact that it simply wasn't easy coming to terms with the idea that I was no longer a married woman. I'd worn a wedding band for thirty-eight years of my married life and kept it on for a year after Aaron passed away. Even then I didn't keep it off all of the time. To this day, I still wear my wedding band when I go out if I am so inclined. I wear it with one of the other rings that Aaron gave me over the years. He never gave me an engagement ring, but as time went on, he more than made up for it.

I went online and read that there was a significant increase in baby boomers dating online. There were several sites for my age group, and they all touted their success stories. AARP had their own site called perfectmatch.com. There was also seniorpeoplemeet.com. I certainly wasn't going to register on highlifeadventures.com since hang gliding and rock climbing are not my kind of thing. I also found ourtime.com and olderdatingonline.com. There were some cougar websites, but I wasn't interested in younger men. I wanted someone age appropriate. The only site I even considered registering for was youmustlovedogs.com.

I finally agreed to take the leap of faith when a good friend of mine fixed me up on a blind date. Suffice it to say that as the date became closer to a reality, I grew more than a little nervous. Finally the day arrived. I was a nervous wreck. I pulled myself together and dressed in something simple but elegant. I put on my face and made sure to draw on a smile.

The date was supposed to be drinks and dinner, but I ended the evening after just half a glass of wine. Here's where the protection of the guilty begins. Let's call him "Oscar" because he was like an octopus and that is a good name for an octopus. Oscar just couldn't keep his hands off of me. Oh my god. It was so horrible. Really, it was as though he had eight pairs of hands. After what felt like a very long forty-five minutes, when I finally realized that Oscar was too affectionate for me, I finally pushed my chair back from the table.

"I'm sorry, but you know what? This really isn't going to work for me." I stood up, smoothed out my blouse, which looked like it had been man-handled, and then I left the restaurant. He was a doctor, so it made sense that being out with him was practically like undergoing an examination.

Okay, so it wasn't beginner's luck, but at least I was out there. Another one of my girlfriends became my cheerleader and refused to allow my blind date with Oscar derail me. She fixed me with up with "Larry." Larry actually sounded very good. He was seventy, educated, and a professional. Like me he had also lost a spouse. I happen to have a friend who's in the FBI, so I asked him to do a background check on Larry. After Oscar, I figured I couldn't be too careful. It was my version of Googling someone. It turns out Larry was really seventy-five. I wondered why a man would lie about his age. Could I trust a man who lied about his age? I guess we're all entitled to shave off a few years when we get to a certain age, and, I have to say, Larry looked good for seventy. He looked even better for seventy-five.

We went to dinner, and even though it was our very first date, I could tell that he was very into me. In fact, I had a sneaking suspicion that he could see me as his next wife. My womanly instincts told me Larry was the kind of guy who wanted to be married. He wasn't dating to date. He was looking for a wife to share his golden years with. I knew from experience that widowed men don't do as well alone as widowed women. It was sweet. Then again it also made me uncomfortable because I just wanted to date.

After Larry and I went to dinner a couple of times, my friend Nancy's daughter, Whitney, sat me down. Whitney was twenty-seven years old. This wasn't a friendly chat. It was "the talk." Even my mother and I never had "the talk." Whitney felt it was essential to bring me up to speed on the brave new world of dating. She explained that dating wasn't the same as it was when I was dating Aaron and before I dated Aaron. I told her I had already figured that out. She told me bluntly she wasn't talking about dinner and a movie versus dinner and dancing. She bluntly said that before there was any sex, I really needed to ask my intended for a health report.

I suddenly felt like a dinosaur in a sex education class. A health report? I was supposed to ask a man I barely knew for a health report? Oh, and we were already talking about sex? I was still dealing with the notion of just *kissing* another man that wasn't Aaron. This jogged my memory and brought to mind the days when people warned that you could get mononucleosis from kissing a boy.

How times had changed.

A kiss really is the most intimate thing. The other is just an act that anyone can do. For a woman, at least for me, intimacy in bed is not nearly as personal as a kiss. For women, it's always the foreplay that's more exciting. For men, it's a whole different story.

When I did finally kiss Larry, it just wasn't the same as what I recalled when I kissed Aaron for the first time and so many times after that. Now I'm not saying I didn't feel a little "you know" . . . but it wasn't the same kind of "you know," and I wasn't expecting the kiss to feel the same. To tell you the truth, I think I felt a little guilty that I was kissing somebody else at all.

Back to well-intentioned Whitney and her lecture on the birds and the bees and health reports. She really was so protective of me and clearly wanted to help me protect myself in more ways than one. She went on to say that not only did I need a full health report from my date, but even if I were presented with a clean bill of health, he also still needed to wear a condom. I was just appalled. I had only had sex with two men and I had been married to both of them. I mean, wasn't it bad enough that I had to ask a man for a health report? Now and possibly worse, I was supposed to ask a man to wear a condom? At that point, any suspicions I had about the difference between old dating and new dating were confirmed.

Apparently in the world of middle-aged dating in the twenty-first century, if you have dinner or drinks twice, it's almost expected that you jump into bed with one another. Oscar the Octopus measured progress by the drink, and he had a one-drink rule. Here's the thing: I'm not naive and if memory serves me correctly, in my day, once you'd been dating for months, yes, the issue eventually came up. Romance sure had changed since the 1960s when love was free and not getting pregnant was the only thing that a girl worried about. Larry and I had only gone to dinner a couple of times and seriously, was I supposed to ask him for his medical report and buy a supply of condoms? I listened to Whitney and took everything seriously, but it all seemed a bit premature at that point.

Well, after two months, the subject did come up with Larry. We were kissing one evening and it seemed clear that things might go further in the romance department. I took it upon myself to interrupt the session. I told him point-blank that I needed him to give me a health report.

Talk about a showstopper. Larry was a good sport, though. Maybe he was more aware of the new ways of the dating world than I was. He sat me down beside him like a child who was about to be lectured. I made sure to give him my full attention. In exchange, he gave me a kind and reassuring look.

"Oh, honey, you don't need a health report from me. I had prostate cancer and my prostate was removed. And besides, I haven't been sleeping around."

That was not the answer I was expecting to hear. Suddenly I heard Whitney's voice loud in my head. I asked him what the removal of his prostate had to do with sexually transmitted diseases. I reiterated that I still wanted a Good Housekeeping Seal of Approval.

Larry got the picture, and within a few days, he had submitted his report to me. His marks were high. He had an A plus. It makes me laugh that although it really is a serious issue, nowadays having sex is like applying for a job. You require everything but the references. Despite Larry's squeaky-clean health report, I still had to deal with the condom issue. I commended Larry for the squeaky-clean report but knew nothing was going to happen unless we used a condom.

I had only bought condoms once in my life, and it was just after Tori was born. The doctor instructed us to have protected sex for six weeks. I went into Aaron's office to remind him.

"So you're going to get the prophylactics, right?"

Aaron was on the phone, as usual, engrossed in conversation. It was clear the task was up to me. I was in a room outside of Aaron's office and I picked up the phone and just called the drugstore. I didn't have the nerve to go in and buy them, so I figured I would just order them over the phone and then someone, or even I, could pick them up in a well-disguised brown paper bag. There I was on the phone with the drugstore when Aaron's assistant came in and sat down next to me. I had to whisper into the receiver with my hand cupped over the mouthpiece so he wouldn't hear me.

"This is Mrs. Spelling. I'd like to order some prophylactics please."

It was all very cloak and dagger, and my whispering was so muffled that the man at the drugstore couldn't hear me. He kept saying, "What? Who is this? What is it you want? Can you speak up?" Finally it was just hopeless, so I just spoke up.

"This is Mrs. Spelling, and I need to buy prophylactics."

Aaron's assistant got a little bit squirmy and looked the other way. You can imagine how mortifying it was for me to buy condoms as newly single woman when I couldn't buy them forty years earlier as a married woman who had just had a child.

Times have changed in more ways than one. Now that we need the condoms on dates almost in the same way we need breath mints, it's harder to buy them anonymously. You can't just pick up the phone and call your neighborhood drugstore anymore. You can order them online, but I worry about what kind of spam would start filtering into my inbox the instant I place an order for condoms.

The more I thought about it, the more I thought it might be time for me to take charge of my life and walk into a drugstore and buy them. I mean, I had learned to use a computer, an iPhone, and an iPad. Maybe this was just part of being a modern woman?

To say I was in a panic as I walked into a mega-pharmacy on La Cienega Boulevard doesn't quite capture it. I wanted to be far enough away from home that nobody I knew would see me. I also hoped this wouldn't be on those moments where somebody walked up to me and asked, "Aren't you . . ." Maybe I should have worn the trench coat, fedora, and sunglasses with the fake nose after all.

I waited until there was no one else around me and finally found my way to the condom section. I was absolutely stunned that there was what seemed like an entire aisle dedicated to condoms and other male and female intimacy products. It was overwhelming. It was no different than buying shampoo.

Shampoos for normal hair, dry hair, oily hair, normal to dry hair, normal to oily hair, straight, curly, more volume, taming, color guard, even shampoos that make your hair grow.

As far as I could tell, it was the same thing with the condoms. There were so many varieties that my head was spinning. Latex, lambskin, polyurethane. Different strengths, sizes, textures, shapes, and I won't even go into the novelty choices and colors. I was a "Breck girl," so I had no idea what to buy. I suppose I could have called Whitney since she was my advisor, but I felt that I needed to ask a man. I dialed my son from my cell phone. It all came pouring out in one long, breathless sentence.

"Okay, Randy, you've got to be a big boy about this. I'm about to tell you something and it's going to sound a little scary but I need to buy condoms and I don't know what kind to buy but I'm in the condom aisle at the drugstore and I can read you the labels and you tell me what I should get."

I can't even begin to tell you how uncomfortable Randy was. I wasn't even sure he was still on the phone until I heard him take a very deep breath and sigh. He agreed to help me. I could tell he was implementing the "don't ask, don't tell" rule. With my cell phone cupped in my hand, I started at one end of the aisle and began to work my way through all the packages. I read all the descriptions to Randy out loud while he listened in silence on his end of the phone. Reading the descriptions for the condoms was as tough as reading a contract or blueprints. I can read contracts and line drawings and understand them easily at this point in my life, but all those different condoms were another story. When you consider I was reviewing them with my son, it added another dimension to what was happening on that aisle of the drugstore.

I tried to be clinical as I moved across the shelf. Randy was quiet until I got to the ones that said something like "Magnum Large Size."

"No, Mom. That's not good. Not good at all. That's not what you want to buy. You could make a guy feel really bad if you bought those."

I can't remember exactly what kind Randy told me to buy. I waited until the line cleared at the register and when I handed them to the clerk, I tried to act very casual and matter of fact about the whole thing as though I bought condoms every day. Then I skulked through the parking lot and got in the car. I was exhausted. Getting ready for a date sure wasn't just setting your hair in rollers like it used to be.

I have to give Randy a lot of credit. He really was terrific about the whole episode. A few days later, he even called and asked how everything "went." That was a big deal for Randy, especially because I'm convinced that my two children believe that I had only had sex twice in my life. I guess your kids are just your kids regardless of how old they are.

Larry was way more ready than I was to hop into bed. I kept trying to put him off. "No, it's too soon. I need more time."

It was a good two months before I was ready. I realized that I was with a decent guy (with a clean health report). I was ready to take the plunge and I was armed with condoms.

Despite the fact that Larry passed the health report, he had one caveat he wanted to explain. As it turned out, it wasn't just that Larry had his prostate removed. Larry also had a penile implant. I learned that sometimes when a man has his prostate removed as Larry had, he can't perform the way he did prior to the surgery. I also learned that there are different kinds of implants. Larry's penile implant was the inflatable kind. He explained the mechanism to me, but I still didn't quite understand it. Even though I searched the Web afterwards, I still couldn't figure it out exactly how it was going to work. Honestly, the best way to explain it was "pump and dump." Once I told my girlfriends about his condition, "Pump and Dump" became his nickname.

Larry didn't really talk about the situation too much, but he did say it was very expensive and he was glad he could afford it. I have to admit, it was rather strange. Here I was having sex for the first time since I had become a widow, and I was with a bionic man of sorts. The penile implant may have been great for Larry, but it was horrible for me. My bionic man could go on for five or six hours and there is no woman, middle-aged or otherwise, who wants to have sex for that long. It was like running a marathon. I can't believe it took six months, but there finally came a time when I decided that I didn't want to date Larry anymore. Actually, it wasn't because of the implant but simply because he was getting too attached, and I didn't want to feel attached to anyone.

Another reason that I broke up with Larry was that sex was such a big deal for him. He was insatiable and I just couldn't take those six-hour romps anymore. Larry was a kind, sweet man, so I felt badly when I broke up with him. While we were dating, I had had surgery for carpal tunnel syndrome, and he came to visit me while I was recovering. He brought me candy and flowers. He was a really good guy.

I was right on our first date when I felt that he was looking for a wife. Larry ended up getting married a couple of years after we broke up. I'm glad he found someone and I hope she's not too exhausted.

I moved on from Larry and wound up having a brief relationship with "Not-Curious George." George and I did not get off to the best start. It seemed promising at first when he drove to my house, picked me up in his nice car, and then drove me to a cozy little restaurant on Doheny Drive. When we got to the restaurant, George did something I had never seen done before. He brought his own bottle of wine in a little drawstring sack and handed it to the maître d'. I had no idea that people could bring their own special bottle of wine and pay a corkage fee for having the server open the wine. I've learned that sometimes the corkage fee is more expensive than the wine, and sometimes it's less expensive. I wondered, was George a wine snob or was he too cheap to buy a bottle of wine from the restaurant's wine list? Neither scenario was particularly appealing to me.

It also struck me as a bit controlling. What if I had wanted to order a glass of wine off the list or what if I didn't enjoy wine? George's wine turned out to be a red wine. I wondered if I should act more appreciative of the wine since he had gone to so much trouble.

A million questions ran through my head that evening. I am almost certain that no questions ran through George's head at all. George was nearly silent as we sat at our table and the server opened his wine and poured it for us. I found myself making all of the conversation, maybe overtalking to compensate for his lack of talking. Because it was our first date, I thought George might be feeling shy. I thought for sure he'd comment on his wine or ask me what I thought of the wine, but that was not the case. I refused to give up and kept asking him questions. After a while I realized he hadn't asked me even one question about myself. By the time we left the restaurant, I knew quite a bit about George: the ages of his children, why his marriage had ended, that he had served in the military, and also what made him choose the profession he was in. I also knew he wasn't the least bit curious about me.

It was quite possible that he had read enough about me online or in the press that he thought he knew me. I also thought I could have been more assertive and asked him, "Why aren't you asking me any questions about myself?" I wondered if a lot of women my age go through the same thing. I went out with him a few more times thinking he might warm up, but he didn't. Simply put, I was bored with "Not-Curious George."

"Stan" was another date. He was a little younger than I was, but only by a year. He was very good-looking, divorced, and like me, had two grown children. Stan clearly was not ready to start dating. From what he told me, not only was his wife abusive during the divorce, but she had also been abusive during the marriage. I did a lot of listening with Stan. He was what they call a "fixer-upper," and I was the transition woman for him. My dates with Stan were not real dates. I was definitely more therapist than dinner companion. I like to think that after dating me, the next woman Stan dated had it easier.

I also dated "Jack." Like Larry, Jack became a boyfriend. Having a boyfriend is a difficult thing for me. I'd found that out with Larry, but I had learned and matured since dating Larry, so I wanted to give it a chance with Jack. In the beginning of the relationship, I liked Jack enough that after a couple of months, we spent a long weekend in Mendocino. We were away for only three days, but I still caught cabin fever. There was just too much togetherness. In fairness to Jack, when I was married, Aaron wasn't home much during the day, and when he was, we were always in different parts of the house until dinner.

Even though Jack and I had a suite, it had an open floor plan, so you could see the bathtub from the master bedroom. I realized then I wouldn't even be able to relax in the bath and have some privacy. I suddenly became homesick for my bathroom at home. I thought of Aaron (of course!) and how discreet he always was when it came to bathrooms and privacy. He would always go in the bathroom, lock the door, and run the water. That was a habit he never broke. I suppose if I had asked him why he did it, he might have been in analysis for the next thirty years. Until I went away with Jack, I had never been in a bathroom with someone. Even when we lived in a house with just one bathroom, Aaron and I gave each other privacy.

I liked Jack so when he suggested we go away again together, I agreed. This time, I made all the reservations, put the room on my credit card, and made sure the suite had a second bathroom just for me. Unfortunately, the relationship started to deteriorate after that second weekend away together. Unlike George, Jack was too curious. The questions never stopped coming. I felt like I was being quizzed. Then I noticed that Jack asked me the same questions over and over again to the point at which I started to wonder whether he had Alzheimer's. The more comfortable Jack became with me, the more opinionated he became. He had something to say about my children, my grandchildren, and my friends. He started getting "in my face," as they say, whenever we talked about my life.

The final straw with Jack came when he slept at The Manor for the first (and only) time. It was weird to say the very least. I still had Aaron's photograph on the table of my bedroom. I wasn't hiding or changing anything. The only thing I was sort of hiding was Jack. Some of my housekeepers had been with me for twenty years and of course knew Aaron. I had tucked the condom box in the very back of my closet, but I was still feeling very paranoid and worried that when they were dusting or vacuuming, they would find the box with one condom missing. I was so relieved when I got the idea to reseal the box with my glue gun.

The next morning I did such a good job with the glue gun that the box of condoms looked factory sealed. I left my gift wrapping room and went straight to my bathroom. I figured Jack was probably showering in the other bathroom. Imagine my surprise when I found Jack being served breakfast from a tray in my bed. He looked like the King of England as my butler tended to him. I couldn't believe what I was seeing. Not even Aaron did that. I liked Jack but it was hard to get that picture out of my mind.

My dating life was very active for a couple of years. At one point my girlfriends teased me that I was a femme fatale because I was dating so many men at once. It's true that I was, but I wasn't intimate with more than one man at a time . . . well, except for one time. It was at the tail end of my relationship with

Jack that I met "Richard," and I entered what I refer to as my Samantha Jones period. It didn't last long. Dating two men and sleeping with both of them didn't come naturally to me. Richard was a really lovely guy with one exception: his brain had never recovered from the 1960s era of sex, drugs, and rock 'n' roll. His brain was fried. I liked Richard and he was mad for me, but he seemed like he was still on drugs. We stayed friends after I broke it off.

My driver, William, witnessed most of my breakups because I was usually in the car when I called them. The truth is, it was much easier to break up over the phone. I know it was gutless, but I just couldn't do it in person. Maybe it was because I did it on the phone that they didn't take me seriously. No matter what I said or how I said it, they just didn't believe me. It didn't matter who it was, they always called me back within ten minutes to ask if my "breakup call" was just something I felt in the moment. Even if the initial breakup went well, in the end they all went downhill from there. One afternoon, William was just as frustrated as I was. He glanced at me in the rearview mirror.

"Mrs. Spelling, what is it that these men don't understand? It seems to me you were perfectly clear."

Someone I've known for years called recently to ask me out. He's a prominent well-to-do guy in Hollywood circles. I also know his ex-wife. We were never friends, just acquaintances who ran into each other at parties. She was always teasing her husband about his toupee and the sound it made as the Velcro pulled apart. She had always joked with the rest of us ladies that she knew when he was coming to bed because she heard the sound of the Velcro tearing. As we chatted on the phone, I knew I couldn't go out with him. The problem was not the toupee—I knew I couldn't handle the sound of the Velcro.

I started dating because it was what my girlfriends were encouraging me to do. I did have some fun, but the reality is, I'm still on the fence. I've become fiercely independent, and right now male companionship is not what drives me. I'm sure my attitude would change if I stumbled onto the right man. It would be nice to travel with someone or have dinner and a movie—no strings attached. For now, I'm happy being on my own and spending time with my dog, Madison. The truth is, I can go days and weeks without talking to the men in my life, but when I'm not with Madison, I miss her.

25

Temptations and Frustrations

rma Bombeck really captured my attitude about food when she wrote, "I just clipped two articles from a current magazine. One is a diet guaranteed to drop five pounds off my body in a weekend. The other is a recipe for a six-minute pecan pie."

When I was growing up, girls and women were supposed to be curvy. Marilyn Monroe, Elizabeth Taylor, Ann-Margret, and Sandra Dee were all curvy. The movie magazines were filled with these voluptuous goddesses, but if I saw the slightest little bit of what we called curves on my body, I thought they were fat bulges. I was definitely closer to Audrey Hepburn and Twiggy than I was to the screen sirens. Except for being well endowed in the bust, I was a wisp of a girl. I was built just like my mother and thought she was beautiful, but I couldn't see my body the way it was. I refused to wear knit dresses because as ridiculous as it was, they made me feel fat.

These days we know this issue is called body dysmorphic syndrome, and volumes have been written about it. Truthfully I think most women in Los Angeles and New York City probably suffer from it. In all seriousness I believe many women are overly concerned with body image. In my case I perceived an imaginary defect in my body. This started in my teen years when, like most other teenage girls, I was very preoccupied with my appearance.

We didn't have these terms when I was a teenager or even when I was a young woman in my twenties and thirties. We simply didn't delve into the psychological reasons behind our behavior in those days. I never analyzed or gave it much thought. I just felt fat even though as a kid I was scrawny. Like most other children, I didn't like fruits or vegetables. I was a picky eater, but I had never met a carbohydrate I didn't like. Back then we also didn't refer to carbohydrates as carbohydrates. French fries were french fries and bread was bread.

I think my emotional eating can be traced back to when I was thirteen and had a tonsillectomy. My throat was so sore, I refused to eat much of anything for about three weeks. I remember I was very dramatic about the whole thing. I lay there in my bed surrounded by movie magazines turning away anything and everything my mother offered to me. Even once my tonsils were out, I swore I would never eat again! I was a regular Sarah Bernhardt.

About three weeks after the operation when my throat was healed, the pendulum swung the other way, and I ate everything in sight. I was binging on carbohydrates. Obviously I was using the food as a coping mechanism. First I deprived myself to feel more in control, and then I was out of control and eating everything.

Lucky for me, I had a fast metabolism, and regardless of what I ate, it didn't affect my weight. I weighed in at ninety-seven pounds when I married Aaron. I normally weighed a hundred but I was living in New York and modeling and I also didn't have my mother's delicious cooking or pantry full of goodies. Even though I was modeling, I still didn't feel good about my body.

I always thought "eating for two" when you were pregnant was an old wive's tale until I got pregnant with Tori. I had terrible cravings for salt, and every day I returned to my high-school haunt, Delores's Drive-In on Wilshire and La Cienega. I would park the car and then go in and a order a JJ Burger, which was two hamburger patties with three pieces of bun, shredded lettuce, tomato, and pickles. It was slathered with what they called "Z Sauce," which was like a tartar sauce. I ordered mine with ketchup and mayonnaise and asked for an order of Susi-Q's on the side. The Susi-Q's were the original curly fries you see at burger places today. I washed my whole pregnancy meal down with a Coca-Cola. The most incredible thing was that I didn't gain my first pound until I was in my second trimester.

Once Tori was born, I got even thinner than I had been before I was pregnant, and after Randy was born, I was back in my pre-pregnancy clothes just a couple of months later. Aaron always thought I looked terrific, but I still couldn't see how I really looked.

When I got into my forties, I began to gain weight just like most women tend to do. That was the first time I had to start watching what I ate. The weight gain wasn't that big of an issue because I wasn't eating emotionally the way I had when I had my tonsils removed at thirteen. It was when Aaron was diagnosed with prostate cancer that it was clear I was turning to food for comfort. I chose to ignore it and bury my head in the sand, but unhealthy patterns in my eating were developing. I had this terrible habit of eating late, just about an hour before I went to bed. It's awful for your digestion. Unfortunately, I learned it from my mother and passed it along to my son. When I was younger, it didn't matter because it was just my routine, and it didn't bother me because I didn't gain any weight.

Well, once Aaron was diagnosed with cancer, eating before I went to bed became almost an obsession. I was stuffing my feelings with food. Aaron wasn't feeling well and wasn't up to getting out or having people over. Unless it was an event or a dinner I needed to attend for the sake of business or appearances, I didn't go. While Aaron was resting or sleeping, I found myself either shopping for collectibles online or eating. I was stressed, frantic, worried, and terribly bored.

I suppose I could have read a lot of books or taken up a new hobby, but honestly, when you're stuck in all those feelings, it's hard to break a negative pattern. I was always someone who loved projects and hobbies. Somehow, eating had become my hobby. Food filled the black hole that was swallowing me up alive as I struggled to come to terms with the fact that Aaron was sick.

Once I started going to therapy and discussed it with my psychologist, I realized I had body image issues and that I was eating to comfort myself. Until that day, I had never really discussed my issues with food or my body with anyone. It honestly was a revelation. I always figured that was just the way I was. I was a double Virgo, so I was critical of myself.

I didn't start therapy to discuss my issues with food. I just happened to be giving her an overview, explaining that I found myself eating to excess at all hours of the day and night. She explained that people eat to soothe themselves when they're stressed, bored, lonely, or unhappy. Because comfort foods are usually high in calories, you gain weight quickly. I was eating bread with butter, entire bags of Pepperidge Farm Goldfish or Cheez-It crackers, and sandwiches piled high with salami. I had new things all the time. Then Randy introduced me to chicken wings, and I found out you could get those delivered with pizza, so that became my thing for a while.

My therapist and I talked about eating as a way to fill in the emotional hole that I had in my soul. The hole wasn't just about Aaron's illness. It was much older than that. It went way back to my childhood and the ways in which I was programmed to be perfect.

It was hard to hear, but it was all true. Eating replaced so many things that I wasn't facing up to. It was a way of avoiding what I really needed to own up to and tackle. I suppose it was another way of compartmentalizing. I gained quite a bit of weight. It was so frustrating because eating was the only thing that made me feel happy and satisfied. At least it was in that moment.

Afterwards, I always felt terrible about myself. I wish I could have shared my feelings with my girlfriends, but I didn't want to sound like I was complaining. I also just wasn't at all comfortable sharing those sorts of personal issues, even with people I was close to. Thinking back on it, it makes me sad.

It was no coincidence that my issues with food flared at the same time Aaron got sick. I felt so out of control, not just with food and my weight but with so many other aspects of my life. I felt particularly helpless when it came to my husband's illness. It was a vicious cycle: eat because I'm depressed, and then I became depressed because I was gaining weight.

I went to see Hermien Lee when I first began putting on serious weight. Hermien was a prominent nutritionist who died in 2009 at the age of ninety-two. According to her obituary, she took a fall while visiting family in Nashville, Tennessee, over the Christmas holidays. She broke her elbow and her hip and needed surgery. It was after her operation that she had a heart attack. It was sad but still, she made it to ninety-two. Her health regimen must have been a good one.

Hermien was so insightful. She completely understood what I was going through. She knew all about the psychological reasons for an attachment to overeating. The first round of sessions with Hermien worked for me. She worked out a nutrition plan for me and held me accountable when it came to sticking to it. I listened to her, followed the regimens, and lost the weight. Then I gained it right back. I went back to see Hermien, and this time she passed along some tricks that she used when she was very heavy. First of all, she admitted that she had replaced her eating with seventeen-hour workdays so that she barely had time to eat. Well, I was just sitting at home worrying about my sick husband, so working harder was not an option. That's when Hermien gave me what she thought was a great psychological device.

Hermien's downfall was always chocolate cake. She explained that in order to stop craving and eating chocolate cake, she envisioned a big, disgusting cockroach embedded in the chocolate cake. It repulsed her so much that even if the cake was right in front of her, she wouldn't and couldn't eat it.

I gave the cockroach trick a shot. The problem was, if I pictured the cockroach in my comfort food—let's say it was a chopped liver sandwich—I just pictured myself eating around the cockroach, no problem. When it comes to dieting, everybody is different, and you have to do what works for you. The second round with Hermien wasn't helping, so I figured I would just give it a try on my own.

The first thing I did was just cut down on my food. I really kept track of what I was eating and stopped with the late-night eating. I made a point of eating dinner three hours before I went to bed and not one hour. Exercise was an obstacle for me. I have never liked exercising, and even though I didn't exercise, for most of my life I had a perfectly flat stomach. I didn't have any real core strength, however, which isn't good for the back, especially as we age.

I developed back-pain issues when I was fifteen. Of all things, I was taking a driving lesson and got rear-ended. My instructor was badly injured, and I was also treated in the emergency room. The doctor said that they didn't want to do anything surgically until I was an adult. I was only a teenager, so I didn't take it seriously. Youth makes you feel invincible. It wasn't until after I'd had two children that I started developing serious back problems. I had several back operations, including a procedure to fuse my discs, but I still have back pain.

For a long time, I used my back problems and more recently my carpal tunnel syndrome as an excuse not to exercise. If I'm being really honest with myself, the truth is, I didn't exercise before the car accident. I have such a mental block about it that I didn't even try to find a way around it.

I started planning walks and pictured how lovely it would be to walk down the beach in Malibu. I tried my best not to focus on the pain I felt when I walked on the beach and what hard work it was to trudge through the sand in tennis shoes. It was hard for me to stay motivated, and just as I was about to slip on my sneakers and get outside or jump on the treadmill, I was so depleted from the mental exercise of staying positive that I was too tired to walk.

I thought about motivating myself by setting an exercise date with a friend so that I would be accountable. I had had success with that in the past. But then all of the mental gymnastics started again, and it all got very complicated in my mind.

Aaron was not athletic either, but he liked to bowl and play tennis. I'm not a great tennis player and I also didn't love it, but I learned because it was important for us to play doubles and network with other people in the business.

I didn't have that competitive edge, so I was grateful when we stopped playing doubles.

It all came down to being truthful with myself. I didn't want to exercise even though it's good for my health. My regimen with Hermien failed because it wasn't and isn't about food. It's about resolving feelings. My relationship with food and my ability to discuss my feelings are a work in progress.

Last year, Tori dedicated her lifestyle book, *celebraTORI,* to me. The dedication was very sweet: To my mom, the master party planner. I learned everything I know from watching you throw the most amazing parties with so much love. Thank you for the gift of knowing it's all in the details. I hope my parties make you proud! I love you, Tori xoxo

Not long after, Tori also wrote me a beautiful letter in which she shared that it was painful for her to hear how critical I am of myself. She is right and I know I need to learn to be compassionate toward myself and be forgiving of myself. It's really hard.

Tori was trying to set me up on a blind date with the father of a friend of hers who had also lost a spouse. I looked him up on Google and saw that he was very handsome and extremely fit. I e-mailed Tori back.

"Did you tell him that I'm fat and one of my hands doesn't work very well?"

"He saw you on HGTV, Mommy. He thinks you're beautiful. You *are* beautiful."

It was music to my ears, but instead of absorbing what she was saying, I thought, children have different eyes for their parents.

That's just the kind of thinking I am trying to stop. Take today, for example. Instead of being hard on myself about the number on the scale, I am trying to focus on the fact that I walked on my treadmill last night and also did my exercises in the swimming pool. That's quite an achievement for me.

Aaron once said to me that Elizabeth Taylor couldn't stay married because she was too high maintenance. I find that since I entered my sixties, high maintenance is a necessity but not in that Elizabeth Taylor way. They call these years the "Golden Years," and yet so far there is nothing golden about them.

Let's face it, food doesn't metabolize the way it once did, and when I gain weight, I seem to gain it everywhere now. It starts in my middle section but then seems to slide all over the place. My soft midsection is a new creation of the last five years or so. My chest is a medical mystery. Even though I had a breast reduction years ago, "they" seem to have made a comeback.

When I turned fifty, I was actually convinced I could lose weight as the hair was removed from places it never grew before. I have to laugh because one day you wake up and everything has changed. Some women suddenly notice they have the beginnings of a beard or mustache. Not even my feet look the same, and I have pain in places I didn't have it in before. I feel like I am at war with Mother Nature.

It's hard because there is such a double standard for middle-age women. Men can be overweight or bald, and they're still considered attractive. Women, on the other hand, are held to impossible standards of beauty.

That being said, it sounds corny but beauty really does come from within. I have had my share of maintenance done, but I refuse to go crazy with Botox or collagen. I think a lot of women have taken the plastic surgery thing too far. I've actually had to stop friends from having too much done. And I can't believe I'm saying this, but there are many women my age who would look better if they gained five or ten pounds.

I'm learning that our attitude is the most important thing. I need to be happy with what and who I see in the mirror. Regardless of what I do cosmetically and surgically, I have to be happy on the inside because if I'm not, then I won't like the reflection looking back at me.

26

My Story with Tori (and Dean)

Tori and Dean walked into Aaron's service and took seats in the back row. It was very emotional for me to see her because I didn't know if she was going to show up. This was my first time seeing my new son-in-law, Dean. It was very uncomfortable. A friend of mine couldn't bear the awkwardness.

"This isn't right," he said. Thankfully he got up out of his seat and brought Tori and her new husband to sit with the family.

The day was starting to remind me of my father's funeral. After my mother died, my father met his new wife on the set of *The Love Boat*. At his funeral years later, my father's wife refused to let me sit with the family.

My father had remarried a few years after my mother passed away. There was a significant age difference between them, but who was I to throw stones considering the age difference between Aaron and me. They were still age appropriate for one another and they seemed happy in their new life together.

After they were married, they bought a house in Westlake Village. Once again, my father was living beyond his means, and yet again his wife had no idea. This all came to light in 1994 when my father passed away at the age of seventy-seven. Because of all his debt, his wife was not able to stay in their home and had to put it on the market. She asked Aaron and me to buy her a new house.

Aaron and I discussed it with our attorney and our business manager. They both strongly advised us against it. They felt strongly that this was one of those situations in which if we were to buy her a house, we would end up supporting her for the rest of our lives. We decided to compromise and offered to purchase her a condominium instead. She rejected our offer and refused to speak with us again. To this day she has all of our family photo albums and personal effects from childhood in her possession and refuses to return them.

There were lots of mourners at The Manor when I got back from the funeral. Randy, Aaron's brother Danny, his nephew, his niece with her husband and kids. It reminded me of being a bride. For hours you are surrounded by these happy faces smiling at you, only this was the opposite. Everybody was somber and looked at me with grave concern. Time seemed to stand still as I noticed certain faces: Larry and DeeDee Gordon, Bill Haber, Lew and Willy Erlicht, Arline and Henry Gluck, Michael and Ernestine Young, Eli and Nancy Blumenfeld. Tori and Dean were there too.

I welcomed my firstborn with a big hug, but we still couldn't hide how uncomfortable we both were. This was the first time I could remember seeing her since her postwedding brunch at the Bel-Air Hotel after her wedding to Charlie.

Dean was polite but made a point of acting protective of his new wife. I knew exactly how he felt. After Tori's surprise visit a couple of weeks ago, Aaron repeatedly asked Randy if he'd heard from Tori again.

Aaron and I couldn't figure out why Tori had disappeared after her wedding. Eventually word came through the television grapevine that she and Charlie, who was a writer and an actor, had sold their treatment for *So NoTORIous* to VH1. The show, written by Tori and Charlie, was a comedy based on Tori's childhood. Loni Anderson played me, and in an homage to Tori's father, Aaron was depicted only as an off-camera voice like Charlie in *Charlie's Angels*.

Aaron hadn't had his stroke yet, so he still had lucid stretches. I was devastated about Tori, and he was angry. He left her numerous messages on her cell phone. I tried reaching her as well. Not surprisingly, we didn't hear back from her. One day Tori's assistant, Marcel, finally answered the phone. It turned out that he was no longer her assistant, but he had kept the number.

"This isn't Tori's cell phone anymore, but I can get a message to her." This left us without any way to contact our daughter except through e-mail.

Shortly afterward, we heard that Tori was getting divorced from Charlie and was romantically involved with her co-star from a television movie she had just done called *Mind Over Murder*. Before her wedding, Tori and I had discussed her reservations about marrying Charlie, so I wasn't shocked. I had never shared these mother-daughter conversations with Aaron, so he didn't expect this turn in their relationship. He didn't take the news well at all.

Sometimes before you can go forward, you have to look back. That's something I learned in therapy. With that in mind, I can see that my difficulties with Tori are shades of the same kind of tension I had with my own mother. She was a relentless perfectionist, and so am I. The difference, I suppose, was that my mother and I always spoke to one another. Admittedly, it was more of challenge once I married Aaron and was more focused on building a life with him. It took effort on my part, and there were some days when I would think, "It's been a week since I've spoken to my mother. I'd better call her." I thought of her often when The Manor was under construction. I vacillated between wishing she had lived to see it and knowing she would have found something to be negative about.

I've always said that mother-daughter relationships are even more complex than marriages. The umbilical cord is cut at birth, but I've learned that it's very difficult for mothers and daughters to establish separate identities. I don't believe I was in any way a better daughter than Tori. All mothers and daughters have misunderstandings and fights; it's just not every mother and daughter whose disagreements become headline entertainment news or tabloid fodder.

Less than a week after Aaron died and just days after we buried him, *US Weekly* began publicizing their upcoming cover story. It was an exclusive interview with Tori, and the feature was called *I Never Said Goodbye*. A few days later the magazine hit the newsstands and reported the following:

"On the night of June 23, Tori Spelling sat in Betty's restaurant in Toronto, Canada, when she received the heartbreaking news via BlackBerry that her father, legendary producer, Aaron, had passed away: 'A friend of mine had seen a TV report and e-mailed me, 'I'm so sorry. I just heard your father died.' And I was just in total shock,' Tori tells *Us*. Her sorrow quickly turned to anger.

"'My first thought was, I can't believe my mom didn't call me!' Actually, it wasn't a total surprise since Tori, 33, and her mom, Candy have been in a longstanding feud. Because of the estrangement, the self-proclaimed daddy's girl had only seen her 83-year-old father—whose health had been failing for months—on one occasion since last September."

A month later there was another *US Weekly* feature story entitled *Her Mother's Revenge,* and there I was inset on the magazine cover. Here is an excerpt:

"*US* has learned exclusively that the actress, 33, will get just 0.16 % of the Spelling fortune. Tori's share—'a cash inheritance payment of $200,000, combined with approximately $600,000 in private investments her dad set up for her'—is a brush-off Aaron Spelling would never have intended for his only daughter, says a family source.

"'I believe Candy had a lot to do with what was left for Tori,' the source says of Tori's mother, who is sole managing executor of the estate."

Soon every media outlet had copies of Aaron's last will and testament. There were unfounded accusations that I had revised the will to disinherit my children. I was no longer the Marie Antoinette of The Manor. I had quickly been recast in the role of Shakespeare's Lady Macbeth.

What nobody knew was that both Tori and Randy had already received disbursements from a trust while Aaron was still alive. In the meantime, the press were in copywriting heaven with headlines like *Dynasty in Distress* and *Dynasty Duel*. They also had a ball drawing parallels between Tori and Fallon Carrington.

On July 31, 2006, just over a month after Aaron passed away, Joel Keller of *Huffington Post TV* wrote the following:

"In today's *New York Post,* resident yenta Cindy Adams mentions an article in the September issue of *Vanity Fair* that details the sad last days of TV legend Aaron Spelling, who passed away last month. According to the article, written by Dominick Dunne, Spelling was suffering from Alzheimer's disease, and lived pretty much alone in his 123-room mansion. Apparently no one visited, including daughter Tori, which confirms the rumors that there was a rift in their relationship.

"According to Adams, Spelling would 'dine in pj's, go to bed at 9, had lost control of the company he'd founded and nobody—especially his kid—ever came over. The daughter he'd lived for learned of her father's death on television.' Wow. A guy with all this money and power, who was a major player in entertainment, and he went out with a whimper. It's too bad."

It made me incredibly sad that even Dominick, whom Aaron had considered a dear friend, was hungry for a byline. *Aaron Spelling's Season Finale* appeared in the September 2006 issue of *Vanity Fair.* In his column Dominick wrote, "For years, their marriage has been a topic of conversation. I think of it as an unhappy house, a complicated marriage, and an unhappy family."

In Dominick's version, Aaron was more *King Lear* than he was the Scottish nobleman Macbeth. "Two years ago, with only two programs on the air, after having been the leader of the pack for almost two decades, Aaron was left with little control of his company." Aaron had never lost control of his company, though. As early as 1988, production costs were soaring, so Aaron was already looking ahead and trying to a form strategic alliance with a wealthy parent company. He told business reporter Mark Frankel that production companies like his "would have to branch out and do other things besides just producing for television—become miniconglomerates—in order to make sure that we can keep doing what we do."

Through a series of mergers and leveraged buyouts, Aaron Spelling Productions came to be owned by Viacom. They put Aaron's company on the market, but when it didn't get the kind of bids Viacom was hoping for, they began all their corporate restructuring and consolidation of the different divisions.

On his website, *Head Butler*, author Jesse Kornbluth describes Dominick Dunne as "a professional hater, a scourge of the rich and criminal, a judge with a pen." Apparently, Dominick also didn't keep up with the financial papers.

All kidding aside, it was awful to read what Dominick wrote about Aaron because for more than forty years, Aaron had been had been so loyal to Dominick. When most of Hollywood had turned their backs on Dominick and he was *persona non grata*, Aaron stood by him and helped him earn a living by hiring him to write a couple of television movies.

According to his *Vanity Fair* article, Dominick, who had never been to The Manor, said Aaron "had become a deeply unhappy man, living sick and isolated in the biggest house in town, cut off from nearly everybody, estranged even from his daughter, and fearful that he was being betrayed."

Aside from the fact that the columns written by Cindy Adams and Dominick Dunne were so humiliating to Aaron and hurtful to me personally, they were also insensitive to the millions of individuals afflicted with Alzheimer's, not to mention their families. Alzheimer's is a cruel disease. Just because he was Aaron Spelling, my husband was not spared the horrible, undignified symptoms of Alzheimer's.

I was very concerned with protecting his privacy and preserving his dignity. He was a public figure, and I didn't want him ridiculed. I knew from Nancy Reagan's experiences with Ronnie that this was my job—to protect my husband. Aaron was bedridden but he was never alone. He had nurses around the clock. I was there and Randy was there.

Aaron had the erratic mood swings common with Alzheimer's. He hallucinated and became paranoid as his health further declined. Here is a description from the Alzheimer's Association website, alz.org, about the type of hallucinations Aaron had as he declined:

"These false perceptions are caused by changes within the brain that result from Alzheimer's, usually in the later stages of the disease. The person may see the face of a former friend in a curtain or may see insects crawling on his or her hand. In other cases, a person may hear someone talking and may even engage in conversation with the imagined person."

Aaron's paranoia was something we lived with every day. The Alzheimer's Association summarizes this symptom very succinctly:

"A person with Alzheimer's may become suspicious of those around them, even accusing others of theft, infidelity or other improper behavior. While accusations can be hurtful, remember that the disease is causing these behaviors and try not to take offense."

It was hard not to take what was being written personally. What could have been a platform to create awareness about Alzheimer's disease and support for the families ended up being a media assault on our marriage. I never have figured out why it was so hard for the public to accept that I was named executor of Aaron's will because I was the one he most trusted to manage our estate. We weren't Anna Nicole Smith and her eighty-six-year-old sugar daddy. This was my husband of thirty-eight years.

With time, I've come to understand it better. Tori really is so much like her father. She is very talented and has the ability to capture the attention and imagination of the American public with her storytelling. Much like Aaron, she really has her finger on the pulse of pop culture tastes, and she was able to take our normal family dysfunction and turn it into years of record-breaking ratings in reality television.

It used to be that shows like *The Brady Bunch*, *Family Ties,* and *The Cosby Show* were the big ratings winners. Nowadays there is an awareness that most families are dysfunctional in some way, and shows that reflect this are more typical than the Norman Rockwell tableau created by so many of the scripted shows. We are flawed human beings, and life is complex. I think this is why so many of the reality shows like *Keeping Up with the Kardashians* and my daughter's show, *Tori & Dean: Home Sweet Hollywood,* are so popular.

During the year that we were estranged, it was excruciating not hearing from Tori and not being able to get ahold of her. This was especially true at the Emmy Awards tribute to Aaron.

I can't begin to describe the emptiness I felt inside when Aaron was honored at the 2006 Emmy Awards. It was two months after Aaron passed away. Randy was my date that night. I could see the cameras pan across to us sitting in the audience as we watched the highlights of Aaron's career on the big screen. I don't think there was a moment that I didn't have my handkerchief in my hand. I kept blotting my eyes and blowing my nose. I knew that I was on camera, but I couldn't help sobbing. I didn't even care that my mascara was running down my face on HDTV.

Aaron was at his best in the footage, and he was larger than life in that room at the Shrine Auditorium. The original stars of *Charlie's Angels* made the tribute to him, and when Kate Jackson said she could still smell the cologne Aaron wore, I could too. Looking back on his life and all of his accomplishments was incredibly emotional for me, but it wasn't the only reason I was crying. I was also sad because I knew that Tori was somewhere in the audience, and I wished so badly that we could have all sat together and shared that special moment.

One day women started approaching me on the street to share their own challenges as parents and their stories of estrangement from their children. It was right around that time that the tone of e-mails I received began changing from offensive to empathic. Women from all over the world were suddenly commiserating with me.

We have never discussed that painful period in our lives when we didn't speak. We just tried carefully to move past it. I like to think it was her pregnancy that paved the way for us to resolve our issues. I think it was when she went into labor with her first child, Liam, that we both really let bygones be bygones and skirted right past the elephant in the room.

Tori was in the hospital in labor when the doctor came in and turned off the monitor. Something was wrong: the baby was not in the proper position, so Tori would need a C-section. When she called me, all I remember hearing was "Mommy." I could hear the fear in her voice, so I dropped everything and went straight to the hospital to be with her. I had given birth to Tori a month early, and Randy was almost three months premature, so I remember vividly that terrifying feeling of the baby being at risk.

It was incredible to be there for the birth of my first grandchild. He was such a gorgeous newborn and brought so much joy and peace to our family. It was a wonderful time. That year we celebrated Christmas together at The Manor.

27

Crisis Management

I've always been an expert in compartmentalizing. They say men are usually better at disconnecting thought from feeling, but I'd probably give most of them a run for their money. In my family children didn't speak unless spoken to, and emotions were labeled as something negative, so I learned at a young age to stuff everything down.

We also had a lot of secrets in my family. The big skeleton in the closet was of course my maternal grandfather leaving my maternal grandmother, Helen, for my paternal grandmother, Ada. But we also had a lot of everyday secrets that hung in the air. There were our shaky family finances and the fact that my father was what was known then as a flimflam man. He was a trickster who made at least part of his living by defrauding people. There were also my father's infidelities. The letter I had found in my mother's jewelry drawer as a teenager pointed only to one indiscretion, but even at that age, my instincts told me there had been more.

My mother's depression and unhappiness were also secrets and more important, a topic I never would have thought to discuss with anyone. Probably the most confusing part for me was that I was expected to be so perfect for both of my parents. I had to look the part and act the part. Ironically, the standard was set very low for my brother, Tony, who ended up in military school.

Any good psychologist will tell you that putting all these conflicting viewpoints into separate compartments isn't healthy, and as a solution works only short-term. When Aaron became ill and Tori disappeared, I had limited emotional and mental energy to deal with these crises. I handled each one the best way I knew how—by continuing to stuff all of my feelings down—and I also chose never to discuss either situation with anyone but my therapist.

I didn't have a lot of girlfriends when Aaron was still around. There wasn't any particular reason for this except that I was a wife and a mother, and I just didn't have time for girlfriends. I also didn't like those luncheons where I had to get all dressed up in the middle of the day and make small talk. As we say in Yiddish, I didn't like being *fartootst,* meaning discombobulated.

On the heels of Aaron's throat cancer, my friend Nancy insisted I get a hobby. I was hesitant to leave Aaron, but Nancy was determined and managed to convince me that I needed an outlet. Nancy and I have been friends since kindergarten, and it was Nancy who decided for me that I would start playing Mahjong.

Mahjong is an ancient card game of Chinese origin. It is similar to American gin rummy and is usually played with four players, and instead of cards, it's played with tiles. Nancy led the charge and assembled our Mahjong group that includes my longtime friend Willy Erlicht, whom I met when her husband was Vice President in Charge of Movies of the Week for ABC. Since ABC was Aaron's network, we ended up going on quite a few retreats together, and we became fast friends. Her husband didn't make friends as easily as Aaron did, so that was another perk of our friendship.

Fabienne Guerin became my neighbor in Holmby Hills when we moved into The Manor. Fabienne and her husband lived right across the street from us. After we met, I discovered that Fabienne had been one of the original "Lava Lava" girls from *Fantasy Island*. It seems we were destined to be friends, and when we moved into the neighborhood, she invited us to a party to welcome us. When the invitation arrived, she was quick to call us to make it very clear that the Irmases and the Butlers were not invited, so we didn't have to worry about anybody alerting the media and then throwing one of our gift baskets in the trash on camera.

Fabienne happened to be the president of the Beverly Hills Women's Club at the time, so that's where we all started taking lessons. Once we all learned, we started meeting every week to play. Usually we played at someone's home, but there were times when we would meet either at Hillcrest Country Club or the Los Angeles Country Club.

As comfortable as I felt with "the girls," I didn't discuss Aaron's illness when I was out with them. Even after Aaron died and I was being slapped left and right by the media, I chose not to discuss what was going on. It was good to get away from my troubles for a while, but more than that, I was compartmentalizing, and my feelings about Aaron and Tori did not belong in my "Mahjong compartment."

I don't think it was a trust issue as much as it was that I didn't want to create a lasting impression. What I was going through was without a doubt the big elephant at the Mahjong table, but it never occurred to me to discuss either situation with my friends. The Mahjong was a diversion, and I suppose I wanted to keep it that way.

I learned pretty quickly that there is only so much emotion you can keep stuffing down before it starts to destroy you. One day I was out to lunch with my friend Denise, who works for Range Rover, and her boss, Mike O'Driscoll. I honestly can't remember what was going on at the time, but there were stories in the press making a fool of me yet again, and for some reason this time, the dam burst and I couldn't stop crying at the restaurant. Denise and Mike were so amazing and compassionate. I knew Denise had her own children and understood my pain.

Later that afternoon Mike called me. I was surprised to hear from him, and I was more surprised that he wanted to talk about the public flogging I was allowing myself to take. These were private family matters, and I believed I was taking the high road by not speaking to the press about my daughter. It didn't matter how many awful photographs they printed of me, I had no intention of addressing my personal issues with my daughter with the press. I also thought anything I said would be taken out of context and used for a sound bite or headline, so I chose not to speak at all. I kept hoping some other really big news would break, but the spotlight continued to stay on me.

Mike was absolutely right. I was at my breaking point. He strongly suggested I get a crisis publicist to handle all the public ridicule, but I wasn't entirely convinced. Aaron had a publicist, and Tori had a publicist, but I didn't know what a publicist could do for me. It seemed like anything I said would just sound like I was on the defensive, so I saw no point to that. But despite my reservations, Mike was persistent. He had someone very specific in mind and told me she had created Johnny Carson's character Carnac the Magnificent. I wondered if this woman who had created Carson's "mystic of the East" could make all of this drama disappear. I was nervous about making the call, but then again, anything had to be better than the way I was living.

I don't know what I thought Linda Dozoretz would be like. I guess I thought she would be some tough broad. She was all business as they say, but she was very genteel. She was the originator of the signature thick black glasses later made cool by Tina Fey, and she was always dressed in grays and blacks. There was something about Linda that was very striking. I'm not sure how to describe it except to say I just knew I could trust her.

Linda took me on despite the fact that she was ill and hadn't been looking for new clients. Her mother had taken the drug DES when she was pregnant with her, and as a result, Linda was plagued by very serious health issues. DES was known as a synthetic estrogen that was widely prescribed to women who were at risk of miscarriage. The drug was taken off the market in 1971 when doctors realized the risk it posed to unborn fetuses.

After our first meeting, Linda outlined a plan for me. I was no longer going to be anyone's punching bag. She helped focus attention on my charity work and my civic work as Commissioner for the Department of Recreation and Parks for the City of Los Angeles. She also encouraged me to write about causes and issues that were important to me. It was because of her that I became a columnist for The Huffington Post and TMZ and a contributing writer for *LA Confidential.*

Under her guidance I was elected to the Board of Directors of L.A. Inc., the Los Angeles Convention and Visitors Bureau. I am a native Angeleno and love this eclectic city of ours, so it was a perfect fit for me. I am also one of the few women members of the Los Angeles World Affairs Council, which is dedicated to bringing influential and visionary leaders in international affairs to speak at events in Los Angeles. Margaret Thatcher, Martin Luther King Jr., Henry Kissinger, and David Petraeus are just a few of the individuals who have spoken at their events.

There is no doubt that Linda was a brilliant woman. She was also kind and caring, and she was always there to listen. We became very close friends and spoke every night on the phone, even when we didn't have business to discuss. In refocusing the media's attention on who I really was and not the role I was written into, Linda also reminded me of my own worth.

Linda lost a thirty-year battle with cancer in November 2010. She was only sixty-two years old. She was incredibly brave until the very end. I learned a lot from the courage she demonstrated. She taught me to stick up for myself and not to take anything lying down.

She was the orchestrator of many savvy media strategies for the biggest names in film, television, and sports. She was also on the board of the Doris Day Foundation and got them to donate a beautiful shade and bench to the Laurel Canyon Dog Park up on Mulholland Drive. Then she persuaded me to donate some trees. It gets very warm up there in the spring and summer, so those trees were a nice addition to the park.

Out of all of Linda's masterful strategies, I think she was most proud of that one.

28

My Story with Tori (and Dean), Part II

M y father was a newlywed with a younger wife when we were building The Manor. Appropriately enough, they had both been working as extras on *The Love Boat* when they met. It's not easy making a living as a television extra, so Aaron and I were helping them out financially. We decided it would be better to give my father a real job so that he could feel good about himself. I didn't entirely trust our contractor, so I thought it would be ideal to have my father act as our controller. It would be his responsibility to read the contracts, make payments to vendors, and keep track of the man hours and inventory. I mean, who could be more trustworthy than my own father?

The first sign that I was wrong in my assumption was the pricey Mercedes two-seater my father purchased for his wife. The second was the European vacation they took. Instead of waiting for the next shoe to drop, I did some forensic accounting on my own and found an entire list of financial indiscretions. I never dreamed that my own father would end up taking kickbacks from vendors and misappropriating funds. Not even in my wildest dreams did I think this was possible. After this my relationship with my father was strained, and it remained that way until he passed away.

I have learned a lot about money over the years. My father is a good example of a situation in which I thought I could help solve someone's problems with money. I thought my father's problem was a financial one, but my father obviously couldn't manage his money. He was a terrible overspender. But his core problem was his entitlement issue.

It took me years to get to the topic of money in therapy. I thought I had anger issues, not money issues. Then as I explored my relationship with my children, I realized we had a pattern. When I denied Tori an extravagant purchase, it resulted in radio silence.

It was hard to watch Tori use our latest mother-daughter problem as the central story line for her reality show. I was also the cliffhanger of many episodes. Her book *sTORI telling* also breathed new life into my old role as Lady Macbeth.

I am by no means saying that I am the perfect mother now or that I didn't make mistakes when my children were growing up. In therapy I learned that I was passive-aggressive and that I also had poor communication skills. It's true. The Spellings were a family who didn't confront issues. There, I said it.

There is another truth about the Spelling family. It's probably a truth shared by countless traditional families in which there was one very ambitious or trailblazing parent. As much as Aaron loved being with our children, he was always working, and when he was home, he was very preoccupied. There were times when the kids were playing in his office while he was on the phone. He had absolutely no idea what they were up to. They could have been cutting off each other's hair for all he knew.

I think Aaron's demanding work schedule and also the fact that he was a writer who logged out of reality and into his imagination left us all wanting more quality time with him. I think it set up a competitive dynamic where we all had to vie for his attention.

Having said that, I also believe that there comes a time when you have to stop blaming your parents. I have learned from my own journey that at some point you have to take responsibility for your own actions and attitudes. I made a deliberate effort to look in the mirror and change. That's where the real work is and where the rewards are.

I was in Portland recently visiting my son. He is married to a wonderful woman, and they have two beautiful little girls. Randy is a lot like me, I think. He is more introverted and very sensitive. When I was up there, he brought up something I had done that had really hurt his feelings. It was a big moment for both of us. Instead of blaming me, he told me how I made him feel, and I in turn got to explain myself without feeling defensive. It was huge and I made sure to share with him how happy I was that we could have this kind of communication. I was very proud of both of us.

A couple of years ago, I planned my first vacation since a girls' trip I went on in about 1998. On that particular trip, I had gone to Europe with my friends Paula Meehan and Joanna Carson. We docked in St. Tropez, and while I was walking around, I saw some stunning paintings by a local artist. He was a short, little man with a handlebar mustache and this great big hat. His wife invited me to come upstairs and see the rest of his work.

I got so caught up looking at his collection and hearing about his inspirations that before I knew it, it was eight o'clock at night. I dashed back to Paula's yacht and explained where I had been. I told them about meeting this artist and going to his studio. Well, I suppose that was the wrong way to start the story because they immediately started teasing me about having an affair. They were picturing French actor Jean Reno when really it was more like Danny DeVito.

It was a fabulous trip, but once Aaron got sick, we didn't leave the city limits. Years later, once I was on my own, I finally took a leap and booked a month-long cruise to Europe, England, and Morocco. It was a milestone for me. My first trip as a single woman and the longest time I had ever been away from home. I was excited and nervous.

But after I had booked the trip, Tori unexpectedly got pregnant with my little grandson Finn, and there were some complications that required her to be on bed rest. I did everything I could to be supportive including renting her an apartment so she could be closer to the hospital.

Even though she was stable and in the best possible care at Cedar-Sinai, I was obviously conflicted about going on my trip. I shared my feelings with her one afternoon while I was visiting.

"No, Mommy, I want you to go."

I took my daughter at her word, accepted her blessing, and went on my trip. Before I left, I promised her that at the first sign of any trouble I would jump on a plane and fly home so I could be at her side.

Thankfully Tori and baby were fine when I returned home to the United States. She was still on bed rest, but she and the baby were both stable. She stayed there in the hospital for about sixty days, and then my youngest grandson, Finn, was delivered by c-section. I got to the hospital just after he was born, and there he was in his little bassinet with the most beautiful big full lips. In my day, newborn babies were taken to the nursery. I have say, I think it's very cool that these days the babies are taken straight to their mothers once they are measured, cleaned up, and checked out.

I love and adore my grandchildren, and it's amazing to spend time with them now that they can talk. I have the same feelings for them that I did for my own children, but now I have wisdom that comes with being a grandparent. My husband and I handed everything to our children, only later to realize that pushing up your shirtsleeves and digging in your heels is character building. Aaron had a tough childhood and never wanted to see his children struggle, and neither did I.

I think the best way to explain my perspective is to quote George Clooney's character, Matt King, in *The Descendants*. At the beginning of the movie, Matt explains his family's intergenerational wealth. Matt says that his father wanted him to have "enough money to do something but not enough to do nothing." That pretty much sums up how I feel now.

Randy has really turned out to be a fine young man. It was hard for him to be taken seriously since he was Aaron Spelling's son. He has taken the road less traveled and found his way. I always knew he would. When he lived in Los Angeles, he would read to the kids at L.A.'s BEST, an afterschool enrichment program here in Los Angeles. He also came out and made Christmas ornaments with the kids one year, so it's no surprise he is such a wonderful father and husband. I am very proud of what he has accomplished. I am proud of Tori too. She is as creative, hard working, and as entrepreneurial as her father was.

I do worry about her, though. Tori is capable and tireless. She is a working mom with four children, a husband, several businesses, and lots of family pets. Even with help, she definitely has her hands full. Migraines run in our family, so we are prone to them. Although they are genetic, they can also be triggered by routine stress. She called me one afternoon about this when she, Dean, and the kids had just come back from vacation, and a migraine was picking up speed.

"Tori, have you noticed that when you go away on vacation that you have the best time, but when you come back and take on so much to make up for lost time, you get a migraine?"

"You know, Mommy, you're right."

Mommy, you're right? Mothers don't get to hear those words very often. When we do, we should record them so we can play them as pick-me-ups for all the times when our children think we're idiots. Is there a mother on earth who doesn't feel as if her children sometimes treat her like she doesn't know anything? I doubt it.

Tori and I are a work in progress and probably always will be. I notice that the more my self-esteem expands, the less patience I have for the pursuit cycle she creates when she shuts me out. We have a pattern and until we can break that pattern hand-in-hand, this is going to be the little dance she and I do together.

29

Up, Up, and Away

The rumors that I was selling The Manor began even before Aaron was buried. I hadn't even given it a thought—it was our family home and the place Aaron most loved to be. Initially, I was annoyed by all of the speculation, and I wondered where the rumors were coming from. Usually where there is smoke there is fire, but I hadn't spoken to any realty companies about putting the house on the market or gotten bids from any moving companies, so really there was no fire. Then I realized the buzz about The Manor's being sold was happening for the simple reason that many women who find themselves widowed with an empty nest choose to downsize.

The Manor was definitely a different house now that it was just me. Time crept along at a languorous pace. Even the light that fell through the windows at the different times of the day was unfamiliar to me. The hallways that had once been filled with so much life, not to mention glamour, were empty. The house had gone from being our home to a monument of a previous existence.

For the first time in the twenty-one years that we lived there, I also didn't have a dog. Not long after Aaron passed away, my dog, Annie, died unexpectedly. It was devastating and came as a huge shock. Now there really wasn't anything breathing life into the quiet house.

Annie was a Wheaten terrier mix that Tori had helped me rescue years before Aaron was sick. We had driven a long a way along Southern California interstates that I didn't know existed to the dog rescue where Annie was in boarding. I had seen her picture and read her profile on the pet adoption website and knew she was my dog. I had a very specific kind of dog in mind. I wanted one that looked like my old dog, Gracie. Gracie had been Tori's dog first. She was also a rescue, and from what we could see or hear, she had probably been turned in for barking. Shortly after Tori got Gracie, she started having problems with her homeowner's association because of the barking, so Gracie moved in with her grandparents. She was a wonderful dog. We loved her so much. Annie looked quite a bit like Gracie in her adoption profile picture, so I had been looking forward to bringing her home with us.

Unfortunately, Annie had already been adopted by an older lady. After two weeks, however, the lady had called the mission back and said that the dog was lethargic and ended up returning her. The day the mission posted Annie's photo I saw it online, quickly called, and picked her up. Rescuing dogs is a big commitment. They often come with so many emotional issues that you really have to be prepared to nurture these little souls back to emotional health. Annie blossomed at The Manor, though she was always a little anxious and never got over her fear of men.

As much as I missed having a dog, I really didn't have the emotional wherewithal to bring another one into my life. Running The Manor was a full-time job in itself. In between doing upkeep, I was focused on finding my way.

About six months after Annie died, it was time to think about getting a dog. I decided to get a puppy because after all I had been through, I wanted a dog that would be around for the longest time possible. I didn't have anything in particular in mind. I just knew I wanted a female.

One of my girlfriends was getting a little Cockapoo puppy, so I went with her to look at them. It was out in Orange County, so we met in a parking lot somewhere and then made the drive behind the Orange Curtain. The Cocka-poos were darling, but they just weren't my kind of dog. In another part of the house they also had a couple of Wheaten terrier puppies and there was my Madison. It was love at first sight.

I brought her home around Christmastime, and she brought so much life and energy to The Manor. She was the only dog I've ever had that would go outside and amuse herself for hours on her own. She would chase the birds and get into the pond, and she was always on the lookout for squirrels.

The five years I spent alone in The Manor were long ones. One morning I woke up and it hit me. It was time to let it go. I wanted to enjoy my life, and I knew it would be difficult with the responsibility of The Manor on my hands. Some part of the house would always be screaming at me for attention.

If arriving at the emotional place where I could make the decision to part from The Manor was difficult, the logistics of selling it was even more com-plex. My attorney arranged for us to meet different brokers, whose marketing plans were submitted to Linda and me for review. There were no comps in the area, so it was difficult to set an asking price. The closest thing to a comp is Suzanne Saperstein's Fleur de Lys estate, which was only a few miles away north of Sunset Boulevard on Carolwood Drive. Inspired by the seventeenth-century Château de Vaux-le-Vicomte, Fleur de Lys was built in 2002 and has been on and off the market since 2006. Truthfully, The Manor and Fleur de Lys were apples and oranges. I figured if Fleur de Lys could command an asking price of $125 million, it was reasonable to ask $150 million for The Manor.

With these kinds of estates, you obviously can't hold an open house. So we relied on getting the word out through the media. Linda also came up with a very clever "150 Reasons to Buy The Manor" and I hit the talk show circuit to promote the house. I was on *The Nate Berkus Show*, *The Wendy Williams Show*, and *Entertainment Tonight*. I also did interviews with everyone from *People* magazine to the *Lansing State Journal* in Michigan. It really was a conundrum. Obviously somebody very high profile, not to mention solvent, was going to purchase The Manor. But if that high-profile personality wanted to fly below the radar, then The Manor was not the place for them to buy. I also wanted a clean deal and not a complicated financial transaction. I had one offer from a very viable party, but the terms included a long-term rent back, and that was not what I was interested in.

Believe it or not, there are quite a number of celebrity "looky-loos" who are known for checking out exclusive properties even though they have no intention of buying them. To avoid this scenario, all potential buyers had to be prequalified. It didn't matter who it was, they had to go through the paces. Jeff Hyland of Hilton & Hyland who represented The Manor explained his process to the *Los Angeles Times* very simply: "If they or their party were not on the Forbes list, it was very easy to decline the showing."

After I sold The Manor, I read a quote from one very-high-profile New York City real estate mogul who claimed to have been shown The Manor. Despite the fact that he is on the Forbes list, he didn't qualify and he was never shown the house. In his defense, I will say that these days not even I would qualify to buy my house.

The Manor was on the market for 850 days before it finally sold. I wasn't at all surprised that a twenty-two-year-old British socialite was the buyer. Petra Ecclestone is an aspiring fashion designer, and The Manor was the perfect way for her to plant her flag in Los Angeles. What did come as a shock was the requirement that I had to be packed and out of The Manor in just thirty days. I was game but my conundrum was when to start dismantling The Manor given that there were contingencies that would allow the Ecclestones to drop out of the deal if there was mold, termites, or structural issues. I knew the house was in excellent condition, but I didn't want to start taking apart my bed frame until the deal was final.

The sand started slipping through the hourglass very quickly as soon as escrow closed. What took in essence seven years to create was being decon-structed in a month. It took three moving companies to pack up more than one hundred rooms, and I did quite a bit of the packing myself. One company was solely dedicated to packing up the attic. I had a schedule and a game plan to get us out of the house. Getting rid of things was incredibly hard for me, but I knew that it was necessary. I was moving to a condo, so I had to prioritize.

Everything in The Manor was marked with a sticky note indicating its final destination. "A" was for Auction, "D" was for Donate, "S" was for Storage, and "C" was for condo, which meant it was coming with me. I rented a warehouse for storage and signed a lease on a temporary residence where I would live while my condo was being built. The Century had offered me a special arrangement where I could rent an apartment from them, but it made more sense to live elsewhere for now.

I really have to give it to the movers. They cleverly placed two-foot wood strips on the stairs so that they could slide boxes from top to bottom with men posted on either side to make sure nothing slid out of control. We all worked from dawn until midnight. When I did get some sleep, I dreamt of Styrofoam peanuts, bubble wrap, tape guns, felt-tip pens, and cardboard boxes. It was the definition of controlled chaos with an emphasis on controlled.

When I had put the house on the market in 2008, HGTV, along with some other networks including the newly launched Oprah Winfrey Network, had approached me about documenting my move in a reality miniseries. Who would have ever thought twenty-one years before when we shot video of the grounds and of ourselves breaking ground that moving out of our home would be so public? Had he lived, Aaron never would have sold the house, but I believe he would have understood if he could have seen my singular life. Making a reality show about packing up the house and moving on was an opportunity to pay homage to the most prolific man that television had ever seen.

We shot a sizzle reel for the show, which is a ten-minute video highlighting what the show will look like to the viewers. The sizzle reel is a key tool when you are pitching a reality show. My producer, Stuart, was beyond excited when he saw the final version of the reel. Even over the phone, I could feel his energy.

"We really have something big here."

Given the market and the economy, neither one of us was in a big hurry, and we figured we would shop the reel until we found the right network. Everything was easy and stress free until the day I accepted the offer on the house. I immediately called Stuart.

"We're in trouble. I just sold the house and I have to be out in thirty days."

At the time, we were in talks with OWN, but they had just gotten up and running and couldn't decide whether *Selling Spelling Manor* fit in with their programming. Since we had a new time line, Stuart pitched the sizzle reel to five other networks which were then quickly whittled down to three. Ultimately, we went forward with HGTV. Stuart and I agreed that they had a lot of integrity and the right point of view, and they remained faithful to it.

It was a big self-worth moment for me when I was asked to be made an executive producer of the show. It's different from scripted television in which the creators are often executive producers. As an executive producer, I would have decision-making power, and that gave me a sense of control. The network balked at my terms, but I stuck to my guns and made it a condition. I had learned to stick up for myself and negotiate on my own behalf, something I would not have been able to do just a few years ago. It was a great feeling when they agreed. We found ourselves shooting the first installment before the ink was dry on the contract.

I was a little nervous about being on camera again, but not nearly as much as I had been when I shot *Bank of Hollywood.* I tried to forget that millions of people would be watching the show, and honestly, I did get caught up in the emotions of what we were capturing.

Aaron's office, which was more like a library, was the hardest room to pack up. Those bound scripts and Aaron's typewriter were where it all began. They were the true foundation of the house and our life. I could still remember decorating his office and accessorizing it. I remember wanting it to be absolutely perfect for him. Before I moved out, I had called Tori and Randy to ask them to come by and choose mementos from the house that they could pass on to their children. Tori chose Aaron's typewriter.

I donated all of Aaron's bound scripts, production stills, and awards to the Film and Television Department at Boston University's College of Communication. The school has an emphasis on writing, and I knew in my heart that's where Aaron would have wanted his collected works to go. On October 4, Boston University opened the Aaron Spelling Room, and I was there for the dedication.

For thirty days I had been living in such an abject mess that it was a big challenge for me since order and cleanliness are at the core of my being. I kept talking myself off the ledge and reminded myself that once it was over, I could completely fall apart. In the meantime, there was no rest for the weary because Petra Ecclestone was set to begin construction the morning after I moved out.

When the last day came, it hit me hard. It was an "all-hands-on-deck" situation as my staff, who had been relegated to a tiny work space, cleaned out the refrigerators on the lower level of the house. On the one hand I was looking forward to being out from under the responsibility of The Manor, but on the other hand I was overwhelmed with precious memories. I looked out the window at the pool and remembered when the patio was filled with people. I'll never forget the look on Aaron's face when I told him that I had kept the carpet paid for by the British Commonwealth when Prince Charles came to visit.

"What were you thinking?" he'd asked.

As I walked through the empty house and said goodbye to the bare walls and the empty shelves, it was very intense. I saw the faint imprint of where the pool table once stood, and in my mind's eye, I saw Aaron and a twelve-year-old Randy shooting pool. I pictured Aaron with his ever-present pipe, and I could just about smell his tobacco. I thought of Tori coming over with my grandson Liam and Liam saying the screening room was his favorite room. That told me he was indeed Aaron Spelling's grandson. I ran my fingertips over the floral pattern I had designed for the bedroom so long ago that it seemed like a dream at this point.

What had been our home was suddenly a ghost town. My adrenaline had finally leveled off as I prepared to shut out the lights and pull the door closed.

As I drove my car through the gates one last time, I was letting go of an entire lifetime.

Selling Spelling Manor drew an audience of more than 4.2 million people for HGTV. The special encore night also garnered ratings that placed HGTV in third place for the night. I was truly touched that so many people tuned in. The success was bittersweet, but I walked away with all of my memories knowing that home isn't only where you start off, it's where you choose to go.

30

The Decorator

I always thought it would be fun to do an updated version of Aaron's 1965 pilot of *The Decorator*. The show was a comedy that starred Bette Davis as an elegant and refined Santa Monica decorator living beyond her means. Her character, Miss Lizzy, left threatening notes for anyone who dared wake her before noon and had a stack of "37,000 unpaid bills" that included a delinquent charge for a "beaded evening gown from Saks Fifth Avenue."

Miss Lizzy's assistant, played by the hilarious Mary Wickes, forces her to join the world of the working stiffs. Despite reiterating her belief that breakfast was "for ditch diggers and drum majorettes," Miss Lizzy reluctantly agrees. After that, she goes to stay with different clients every week and decorates their homes based on what she learns about them. I think Aaron was ahead of his time on this one, and his scripted show would have made a wonderful reality television series.

I watched a few minutes of the first episode on YouTube the other day. I really love the innocence of the show. I'd forgotten my favorite line, which

Miss Lizzy says to a child of all people, "Don't be absurd! Everybody needs a decorator."

It really is true, everybody does need a decorator. Interior design isn't always about putting up wallpaper in the dining room or buying an entire room of new furniture. Sometimes it's as simple as recognizing what your needs are. I worked as a decorator for a couple of years after art school for a contract firm. I decorated condos on Fountain Avenue in West Hollywood and model units over on King's Road. We didn't have generous budgets, which taught me to be very clever in my work. To this day, I remember making a painting to hang on a wall, and it was still wet when I hung it the next morning.

During my last handful of years at The Manor, I updated some of the rooms that needed restoring. It wasn't for me, and it wasn't necessarily fun. It was upkeep, plain and simple. It made me think of a time when Aaron was still healthy and a Saudi prince had made an unsolicited offer on The Manor. It was a very serious offer, and I knew with that money I could build another manor for us somewhere else in the city and still have money left over. Aaron wasn't remotely interested, so the Saudi prince sweetened the offer and threw in a Gulfstream jet. I'll never forget Aaron's reaction.

"What would I do with that?"

I never gave much thought to where I would move after The Manor. I'd never pictured myself living anywhere beyond The Spelling Manor. When I finally put The Manor on the market, I knew that in the next chapter of my life, I wanted a completely different experience, so I was intrigued when my friend Alicia told me about The Century.

In their story, "Putting Out The Ritz: When Hotels Go Condo," CNNMoney.com highlighted what they called "a spate of grand old inns being converted to condo residences." It was happening in cities like New York, Chicago, and now Los Angeles, where hotels "such as the St. Regis in Los Angeles's Century City neighborhood, have announced condo conversions."

The *Los Angeles Times* entered the conversation when they ran a piece entitled "Condo Tower Will Replace St. Regis Hotel." In the article, David

Wine, Vice Chairman of Related, the developer who purchased the St. Regis, said, "'What we have tried to do is set a new standard for a building that will incorporate the best aspects of a five-star hotel, estate and condominium' in one site."

I was definitely intrigued. The offices for The Century residences were being marketed as estate living in a condominium. The hotel building had been demolished, but the developer had offices close to the property on Century Park East. I had my attorney contact them without disclosing my identity because usually when I call myself, the price of everything is always significantly higher.

My attorney went to their offices and saw the little model of the building and also the room where the various finishes they had were on display. The next step was to have Related's architect draw up some plans based on my wish list. My priorities included a gift-wrapping room, a pool, a room for my silver, and a china room. I also had this romantic notion of bringing my roses from my rose garden at The Manor with me.

To my surprise, Related didn't bat an eye at my request for a pool or a rose garden. The building was still under construction, so it was very desirable for them to get buyers involved at the early stages. It was even better for them to get high-profile buyers who would garner media attention and help generate more sales.

The Century was a high-rise slated to be forty-two floors high, making it the twenty-second tallest building in Los Angeles. The idea of being up in the sky, floating above the city lights, was magical. Buying the condo was the biggest leap I had taken in a long time. Through my attorney I negotiated a sale price of $47 million for the penthouse floor and the floor beneath it. Not surprisingly, my acquisition of the top two floors made headlines when the *Los Angeles Times* reported:

"The top two floors of a Century City residential tower still under construction have been sold for a record $47 million to Candy Spelling, the widow of TV mogul Aaron Spelling. A $47-million price tag may seem like an enormous sum, but this is all about downshifting in the fast lane."

After we closed the deal, an interior architect from Robert A. M. Stern Architects tried his hand at designing my condominium. I already knew from my experience building The Manor that architects don't think functionally, so it was no surprise to me when I didn't like the ideas presented. Meanwhile, the housing market had crashed and the country was in a recession, so I had my attorneys approach Related about an adjustment on my purchase price. I was actually ready to walk especially since I hadn't sold The Manor yet. I wasn't in any hurry to go anywhere. I was pleased when Related agreed to our terms.

The *Los Angeles Times* ran with the story "Candy Spelling Gets $12-Million Price Break on New Penthouse." In it they reported,

"'Prices were reduced for Spelling and other buyers who made early commitments to the project,' said Susan de Franca, Related's president of sales. . . . As the housing market fell apart, some local real estate observers speculated that Spelling would abandon The Century. 'The rumors have been quelled,' De Franca said. "We are really pleased.'"

After all the documents had been signed and moneys transferred, I went to visit my white box. That's all it was at that point. Just a massive white box. It was also a second opportunity to build myself a completely custom home. At that point, I decided I wouldn't need an architect anymore. He was overthinking everything and making it too complicated. He also didn't know me, so his designs didn't reflect my needs. I knew enough about blueprints and line drawings that I felt comfortable taking it from there on my own.

I did the same thing at The Manor. In that case, I ended up hiring a jewelry designer from Utah who was also a draftsman. His friend designed the kitchen and ended up staying on for a couple of years as my house manager.

Maybe like the Miss Lizzy character from *The Decorator,* I should have had the architect come stay with me for a week; then he would have understood my needs. I know a lot of people still don't understand my passion for gift-wrapping, but I find it very relaxing and creative. Sometimes I'll just go up there to see what kind of decorative bonkers I have in my inventory. Other times, I'll whip up some bows on my bow-making machine.

Another priority for me was having a little beauty room for myself. At The Manor, we had a barbershop for Aaron. I always felt like that was "his" part of the house. Well, now I wanted a "hers" version, complete with hair-washing sink, makeup counter, and salon chair where I could get dolled up for weddings, evenings out, or media appearances.

For the first time in my life, I wasn't trying to please anybody. I wasn't anybody's daughter, wife, or mother. I had raised my children and been the caretaker to my sick husband, so I felt that I deserved to indulge myself. Aaron would have loved all the engineering I had in the works. Televisions hidden behind moving bookcases and the flat-screen television that comes out from under the bed at the push of a button. But there is no way I would have been able to design a pink master bedroom.

While I moved into my temporary residence in Westwood, I assembled my creative team that included my longtime decorator and friend, Robert Dally. I met Robert ages ago when his partner, Peter Shorr, decorated our house on North Mapleton. I always say Robert and I are twins separated at birth. We finish each other's sentences like a married couple, and we speak the same language when it comes to design. Even though we want to kill each other sometimes, we really do have this creative shorthand that enables us to work well together.

Building The Century was very different from building The Manor. It was twenty-one years later and I was a completely different person. This time around, I had so much more experience, information, and resources, so I was able to avoid all of the major mistakes I made when I was building The Manor. Even though the space I was working with at The Century was much smaller than The Manor, I wanted to implement in a "Wow Factor." This I knew would be derived from the details. It would really boil down to finding different materials and creating unique design elements.

They say no home is complete without a hearth, so one of things I had done was have our living room fireplace at The Manor molded so we could duplicate it in the living room of The Century. The artisan who did my fireplaces came all the way from France. He was recommended to me by someone who had done my floors, and then I found out he had done the garden sculptures at the Fleur de Lys estate, so I instinctively knew he was right for the job.

I also wanted to replicate that feeling of grandness created by the *Gone with the Wind* double staircase we had at The Manor. I had actually designed the motif of that staircase and wanted to replicate it in my new home. The problem I needed to solve here was that the condo has floor-to-ceiling windows all around, so I needed a staircase that wouldn't disrupt the view. The solution for this was a floating spiral staircase. I had taken pictures of the double staircase from The Manor and sent them to the manufacturer in Texas.

The staircase was made of steel in Texas and shipped to a warehouse in the San Fernando Valley, a suburban area just outside of Los Angeles. It was then very carefully cut into four pieces so that we would be able to get it up the elevator to the 41st floor. Once it was up there, it was welded together and then installed.

Robert and I took several trips to look for materials and fixtures. I couldn't have worked with any other decorator. Most decorators will bring you four or five samples, but Robert knows I want to see everything. I am always reminded of when I was throwing Tori a birthday party and we were having tablecloths made. I found this darling Raggedy Ann and Andy fabric at Beverly Hills Silks and Woolens. I knew it was what I wanted, but instead of buying it, I spent the rest of the day looking for options and exhausting all other possibilities.

Things haven't changed a bit. If Robert and I are in a showroom looking at fabrics, I go through the wings and look at every single one. There are times when I am being too particular, and Robert doesn't want to deal with me.

"You don't have to be so matchy-matchy."

Showrooms weren't the only place I went for materials. I visited a number of marble quarries and also spent quite a bit of time at The Home Depot. It's always funny to see people's reactions to me at places like that. I think people are always surprised to see me out there riding around in a golf cart, wearing a hard hat. I enjoyed every minute of it.

It was also a wonderful experience to meet so many interesting and creative people. I hired painters and glassblowers and ordered all of my custom-painted switchplates from The Switchplate Lady. I bought all my bronze that I used on my gate and the columns in the pool from a decorative metal arts studio in New Jersey called Firedance Studios. Some of these businesses were really struggling and were thrilled to have the business. It reminded me of the McNaughten Estate in Holmby Hills that later became the Bing Crosby Estate. McNaughten built his mansion in 1933 when the country was in a depression. He endured quite a bit of scrutiny, but other people saw that his construction was creating jobs and stimulating the local economy, and these voices eventually drowned out the critical ones.

The proprietor of Firedance Studios told me himself that he was about to close his doors until I turned up. The Switchplate Lady's business has also grown exponentially after my purchases. The glassblower I used to create the columns for my pool room has also gotten quite a bit of attention. I met her in a showroom at the Pacific Design Center in West Hollywood. It's not that easy to find someone in Los Angeles with a kiln big enough to fire columns that size. The columns she made are just beautiful and are the perfect complement to the etched glass. The whole look reminds me of Lalique.

One of my favorite unexpected finds was the glass that is the backdrop for the water wall in my conservatory. One afternoon I was out looking for marble, and I drove past a shop that had what looked to be a giant slab of brown marble displayed outside. It didn't have any seams and was just incredible. This shop wasn't even on my radar, so I was so very happy to have had noticed it. I had my driver pull over, and then I went into the store. The slab wasn't marble at all. It was glass and was unlike anything I had ever seen before. It looked like thousands of iridescent glass tiles that had been pressed into hundreds of layers. I bought a slab in a beautiful shade of sea-foam green and used it for the wall of my conservatory that has a sheet of water cascading down it.

Another great find that brought the "wow factor" I was looking for was the pink onyx I used in my bathroom. It is visually stunning and, I have to say, creates such a unique look. The lattice work I had done in the conservatory is also very unconventional and creates an incredible amount of atmosphere. The conservatory is enclosed in glass and has skylights, so it feels like you are outside. It is a perfect place to host our weekly Mahjong games. In general, every one of the rooms has its own look, and I am not afraid to mix different periods. In some rooms I've paired Art Deco lighting pieces with antiques.

One of my big money savers was having my existing sofas reupholstered and re-covered. If you have a good frame, there's no reason to buy a new sofa. I even had the arms on some of my older sofas cut down and reshaped to give them a more modern and updated look. I also repurposed quite a bit of fabric from The Manor and used it to create drapes for different rooms in the condo. I got very lucky with the bathtub from Tori's bathroom at The Manor. They don't make this kind anymore, and I was able to extract it and bring it over to The Century to use in my bathroom.

I get so many e-mails every day asking me for decorating tips and ideas. I think the one thing I consistently have to remind everyone of is that you don't have to need to have what I call "pedigree furniture pieces." Believe it or not, I know how to decorate on a budget. When we bought our house in Malibu, we were definitely stretching it. Aaron gave me a budget of $6,000 to do the whole house.

There are so many wonderful online resources these days. I've even bought a couple of wooden headboards for under $200. I've also bought a couple of nice sofas for about the same price. If you know your color palette, I also highly recommend going to The Home Depot. They have everything from blinds and furniture to wall décor and bedding.

Based on the success of *Selling Spelling Manor*, HGTV wanted to create another reality miniseries around designing and building The Century. Filming for HGTV brought on a layer of stress that really took me by surprise. We were on a tight time line for filming and yet we had no control over the obstacles being faced by the construction crew. We had the typical delays anybody building or remodeling experiences. The only difference is that a delay for the construction crew meant a delay on the shooting schedule.

At The Manor our challenge had been to get out of the house on time. At The Century, our challenge was getting in. Truthfully, we could have staged some rooms or cheated the cameras so that we didn't capture the vendors who were still working on the condo. I know this would have made my producer's life much easier, but I am a true perfectionist and didn't want anyone to film anything that didn't meet my standards.

As each room was finished, The Century felt more like my home, but I didn't have more than a few minutes to appreciate it because then we had to get the crew over to film it. That's how it was. We raced to finish a room and then we raced to film it.

What most people don't know is that I took all of the furniture and artwork from The Manor and integrated them into my new home. I think one of the biggest compliments I got was from one of my security personnel who has been with me for ten years. He was very familiar with The Manor, yet when he stepped off the elevator at the finished condo for the first time, he was speechless. He walked around and looked at the artwork, family photographs, furniture, and accessories and recognized them all from The Manor. They were the same pieces arranged differently, so they all seemed new.

Ironically, my master suite was the last room to be finished. It was a long time coming, and I was finally home. I think in my mind, I had imagined a big celebration when I was finally done with what ended up being a three-year journey. I didn't have any energy left for celebrating. Madison and I were both exhausted, so we just went to bed. A few weeks later, I christened my Manor in the Sky by hosting a fund-raiser for L.A.'s BEST. We had about seventy people over for drinks and appetizers. It was very exciting to have my first gathering in my new home.

We shot some footage of the fund-raiser for *Beyond Spelling Manor*. It was icing on the cake when the show, which aired recently, was a top ten–rated show on HGTV. We beat out TLC, Style Network (now Esquire Network), and AMC's movie of the week.

At some point during the construction, I realized that this would be the first time that I would be moving into a new home alone since my L-shaped apartment in New York City. Somewhere along the line, the unforeseen adventure of my life had propelled me forward. Everything fell into place, and I went from being a decorator to the architect of my own world. I never saw it coming, but I was ready for it when it happened.

31

Candy Gram

It's hard to believe that I am the grandmother of six little grandchildren. It seems like just yesterday I was awaiting the arrival of my first grandchild, Liam. Once he arrived, he opened the floodgates for the rest of his cousins to follow. Tori and Dean have three other children, Stella, Hattie, and Finn. Since Tori and Dean have enjoyed so much success in television, I think most of America is very familiar with the McDermott clan. They're really sort of like a modern-day *Partridge Family*.

Randy has given me two precious granddaughters, Sage and Lotus. Sage is almost three, and Lotus turned one a few months ago. Lotus has a very cute nickname; they call her "Lolo." For some reason, the last time I visited, I just couldn't get the nickname right. I kept getting tongue-tied and calling her "Lulu" or "Lola." It was one of those things where I kept worrying I was going to say it wrong and then I did. The kids all know what to call me since I am their "Candy Gram."

Aaron, I know, would have adored these little ones. It breaks my heart that he did not live to see them. They would have been so spoiled by him, and if he were still around, I could see him playing in the pool with them or using movie magic to create the same kind of spectacles he created for our children at the holidays.

I try to spend as much time with all of my grandchildren as I can. Tori and Dean are a real showbiz family, so they travel a lot for work, and it's hard to keep up with their hectic schedules. Back when it was just Liam and Stella, I bought two car seats and had them both installed in the back of my car. It was so much fun to pick the children up and take them places. Before my condo at The Century was ready and I had officially moved in, the children's playroom on the ground level of the building was complete, so I brought the kids with me and we went and played in there. I loved being able to incorporate the kids into my day that way. I was able to check in at the job site and spend time with them.

Another time, Tori let me have Liam and Stella for an extended sleepover at our home in Malibu. I thought of it as their first official "Spelling Staycation." Dean was away in Canada, so it was a good opportunity for Tori to have some time to herself. She was so nervous about being away from her children. It was very sweet. I got a steady stream of texts from her.

"If you need anything or need me I'm right here."

The children weren't sleeping through the night yet, so this was weighing heavily on her mind. I think she was worried that they might not be able to sleep in unfamiliar surroundings or that I might not hear them if they called out. To be honest, I think she was also worried about me.

Here I was looking after two children under the age of five after more than three decades of not being around children. That's a tall order for any woman. Then when you factor in my age, let's just say I could see why Tori thought it was a little too much for me to handle. The kids were out of diapers by that time, but as all mothers remember, sometimes there are those middle-of-the-night accidents. I told Tori not to give it a second thought.

"If Stella has an accident, she has an accident."

I was more concerned about my dog Madison than I was my bedding or my mattress. Madison is very sweet but a little shy, and Stella was more accustomed to dogs that were more outgoing and gregarious. So she and Madison are both a little nervous around each other, and neither one of them wants to make the first move. I wanted Stella to be completely comfortable, so I had Madison sleep downstairs, which is something she hasn't done since she was being housebroken as a puppy.

At that age, the kids thought sleeping in the same bed with Grandma was just the "most fun," so we all tucked in together that night. I think we must have all looked liked three baked potatoes lined up in my king-size bed. At about two in the morning, Stella was sitting bolt upright.

"Grandma! Grandma! Look what I did!"

I started feeling around the sheet, patting it down with my palms, thinking that for sure the bed was wet. Stella knew exactly what I was looking for.

"No, Grandma! I went to the bathroom all by myself and then I got back in my bed all by myself!"

Stella just melted my heart. She was so proud of herself, and I was so proud of her. Those rhythmic ocean waves must have done the trick because both Liam and Stella slept through the rest of the night. In fact, I had to wake them up at ten-thirty in the morning. It's not too often that anyone sleeps later than I do, but they did. We all had such an amazing time. We played in the sand and made lunch. One day we drove out to the Malibu Country Mart and saw a movie.

I had forgotten how many questions children ask at that age and how your attention has to be 100 percent focused on them at all times. By the end of the third day, my batteries were starting to run down, and I wanted to somebody to put me down for a nap. It made me very happy that at the end of our staycation, the kids had gotten so attached to me that they were sad to go home.

That really is one of the most wonderful parts of being the grandmother and not the mother. You get to experience all of the good stuff without the responsibility of parenting. As grandma, I am just the greatest person on earth. The kids love me unconditionally, and they don't judge me.

The tough part of being a grandma is that you have to keep quiet and let your children parent their children. I have to say I am learning this as I go along and haven't quite perfected it. Like any other grandparent, I make mistakes.

One afternoon, Tori and I were both at Stella's ballet class. They were giving a recital that day and Stella was overly excited that we were all there together. I think it was so emotional for her that she suddenly got very vulnerable and wanted to sit with us instead of dancing with her class. She was especially clingy with Tori and just wanted to be held and cuddled. Tori kept encouraging her to get back into class and dance. Stella surprised us all by saying she would go only if she got some chewing gum. Tori didn't think this was a good idea since she would be dancing, and it was also against the rules to chew gum during class.

Well, I just knew that Stella was not going to get herself back in there unless she had some gum. So I very discreetly reached into my purse and broke off not even half a piece of gum and then slipped to it my granddaughter. She was so cute. She knew not to call attention to herself or ask any questions. She knew Grandma was there to give her anything her parents didn't want to. She quickly popped the gum into her mouth before anyone could catch her and then skipped her way back to her group.

A few minutes later, we could all see Stella's little mouth chewing away as she pirouetted and leapt her way through the recital. Tori knew immediately I was the guilty party.

"Mom?"

Tori usually calls me "Mommy." I'm only "Mom" when she is upset with me, so I kept my attention focused on all the little ballerinas and pretended not to hear her.

"Mom! You gave Stella some chewing gum!"

I continued my pretense that I couldn't hear her above the recital music. Then a better strategy came to me. I adjusted my posture to look slightly offended and took in a breath so I could deliver my line with just enough of a little huff, "I don't know what you're talking about."

I'm not the world's greatest actress, so I wasn't very convincing. In all honesty, the way I saw it with the gum was that it was part of what my job as grandmother entails. The day after the recital, I took Liam and Stella to their favorite frozen yogurt parlor, Menchie's. It was so terrific to watch them make their own yogurt sundaes and pile on the condiments. Honestly, their enthusiasm is contagious. Those kids just make everything fun. I'm really looking forward to Hattie and Finn being old enough so that I can indulge them in special time with Candy Gram too.

Randy and his wife, Leah, are incredible parents as well. They have transplanted themselves to the conscientious city of Portland, Oregon. It's a great city with the beautiful Columbia River running through it. It's a large, sophisticated city but with progressive, small-town values. They are raising their kids in a completely different way from Tori and Dean. It's funny to think that Tori and Dean's children are on television and Randy's kids don't even watch television. I have to say I was a bit skeptical of this at first, but after my last visit, I am a convert. My granddaughter Sage is only two, but she must have the vocabulary and motor skills of a four- or five-year-old. She is so articulate and friendly that even strangers she interacts with at the farmer's market or other public places notice it.

What's incredible about both of my children is how much time they spend with their children. They both also married people who are equally committed to prioritizing their children. Dean is a natural at being a parent. He is great hands-on dad. Randy and Leah are also a real team. They both share in the day-to-day responsibility of their children, and it shows. I think this is in large part why Sage is so present and intuitive, and I have no doubt Lotus will be the same way.

I recently violated my own rule about not offering unsolicited opinions to my children. In my own defense, I gave it some thought before I decided to be vocal. I so admire Randy and Leah's hands-on approach to parenting. It is just the two of them without any help, and they are doing it all on their own. Even though they are enjoying it, every minute of their day is occupied. They never get a break and after spending a weekend with them, I worried that they might burn out.

So I got brave and found a gentle way of suggesting they carve out time for themselves and enlist some responsible part-time help. Randy was open and heard me out. I was happy that last week he checked in to let me know that they had found someone they trusted and were looking forward to having some time for themselves.

As a grandmother I have the wisdom of already having been a mother. So when I think about what I want for my grandchildren, I don't just think about the best schools, the nicest clothes, or other material things. I have already set up school funds for each and every one of them so that they can have the very best educations. Apart from all that, my wish for them is that they are able to continue to blossom into the little unique individuals that they already are. If they are sensitive or creative or whatever it is that they are, I hope those special qualities are recognized in them and nurtured. And more than anything, I would like to be a part of that.

When I moved into The Manor in the Sky, I gave Tori and Randy what I like to call artifacts of our family. I kept enough stuff so that all of the grandchildren could inherit a piece of their family legacy. I think people always assume the family legacy is success in show business. Truthfully, I think all of that was just a wonderful by-product of the true Spelling legacy. As I see it, our family legacy is the ability to see it and bring it to life. I want my grandchildren to know that they can write their own life story, and, if they act courageously and overcome obstacles, they can make it happen.

Epilogue

The House That Built Me

One of my favorite yearly traditions has become attending the *Hero Dog Awards* put on by the American Humane Association. It's a black-tie event honoring service dogs from around the country. The evening is filled with celebrities, animal advocates, and dog lovers. They even have a red carpet for the dogs to walk up just like they do at Hollywood premieres.

The service dogs are nominated by people, and then there is a vote to determine the winner. All the stories of the dogs and their owners are incredibly moving and powerful, but only one can win. The dog who gets the most votes is the winner, but obviously in this kind of competition, everybody wins.

Last year, one of my fellow judges was country singer Miranda Lambert. I don't know very much about country music, but I do know this: Miranda Lambert loves animals. She and her organization MuttNation are tremendous supporters of the American Humane Association. I think she probably moved the entire nation to tears during the *Healing the Heartland* relief concert benefiting the victims of the tornado in Moore, Oklahoma. Her song *The House That Built Me* is just so poignant I couldn't stop thinking about the lyrics.

I had never heard the song before the concert. At its core, it's about a woman's identity. The narrator of the song goes back to her childhood home as an adult in an attempt to resolve some feelings.

The song title, for obvious reasons, is very resonant with me. It made me think of being a little girl and sitting in front of our television set and laughing as George Burns and Gracie Allen bantered with each other. I never would have dreamed that one day my husband and I would be friends with this celebrity couple. I've always referred to The Manor as the house I built or the house that Aaron and I built. The truth is, The Manor built me. It defined who I was to the public, and, even though I had never spoken in public, people believed they knew me and I became a controversial figure.

Gracie Allen had a famous quote that I love: "I'm a very lucky woman. I was courted by the youngest, handsomest, most charming, most sought-after star in show business—but I still married George because I loved him." This always reminded me of Aaron. My story with Aaron was very different from Gracie's story with George, but the quote really captured the idea that the human heart is full of mysteries.

For thirty-eight years I was the "better half" of one of the most rarified marriages in Hollywood. It was only when my husband passed away that I came into my own. With my better half gone, I was left to find my own better self. I never felt that I was in the shadow of my marriage. I was happy and proud to be Mrs. Aaron Spelling. I honestly just never thought of life without Aaron, so when it came so soon and unexpectedly, it was as if someone had turned the lights out.

I suppose I could have just stayed in The Manor and been Aaron's widow, but I was determined to forge my own fate and find my identity. Going forward with a new life when you're in your sixties is frightening and wonderful all at the same time. I laugh when I tell myself that I am just grateful when I wake up each morning. I am at a time in life when you hear, "Just be happy you have your health," and as soon as the person has said it, they knock on wood. I am in full agreement with this sentiment. The strange thing is, in my heart, I still feel nineteen.

Since selling The Manor, people will ask me if I miss it or if I would like to go back there one last time. The truth is, I don't. I have my memories, and fortunately I have no regrets or feelings about The Manor or my marriage that I need to go back there to resolve.

Sometimes I wish we had traveled more, but there was no way I would have ever asked Aaron to get on an airplane. He really was afraid of flying, and I am a fatalist. I never would have forgiven myself if something had happened to him on a plane that I pressured him into boarding.

We once took a Princess Cruise to Mexico. This was back before anybody knew what a Princess Cruise was. Dean Martin didn't want us to go. He offered to buy me a brand-new Rolls-Royce if I would let his friend Aaron skip the cruise and stay home with him. I turned down the car. It had been too long since I had been anywhere outside of Los Angeles with my husband.

Sometimes I find myself thinking about what terrible shape Club View Drive was always in. Club View Drive is the street that ran along the west side of our house. It was uneven and had quite a few potholes that never got filled in. When I think about it, it really is a wonderful metaphor for life. There are no guarantees, and there are always obstacles you need to get around.

My biggest obstacle was the identity The Manor had built for me. The public wasn't my problem. I had to divest myself from being the Lady of the Manor and believe in myself the same way I had believed in Aaron all those years ago. I also had to take some emotional risks to create opportunities for myself. In the last few years, I have really challenged myself and gotten out of my comfort zone.

It all started with *Bank of Hollywood*, a show I almost turned down because I was scared to try something new. Since then, I have created many opportunities for myself, and I hope to find many more. Writing books, producing plays, and traveling have all been wonderful, but there is one opportunity I am particularly grateful for. It has come late in the game, but it is without question my biggest treasure. Finally, at long last, it is the chance for me to just be Candy.

"The House That Built Me"

I know they say you can't go home again.
I just had to come back one last time.
Ma'am I know you don't know me from Adam.
But these handprints on the front steps are mine.
And up those stairs, in that little back bedroom
is where I did my homework and I learned to play guitar.
And I bet you didn't know under that live oak
my favorite dog is buried in the yard.

I thought if I could touch this place or feel it
this brokenness inside me might start healing.
Out here it's like I'm someone else,

I thought that maybe I could find myself
if I could just come in I swear I'll leave.
Won't take nothing but a memory
from the house that built me.

Mama cut out pictures of houses for years.
From *Better Homes and Garden* magazines.
Plans were drawn, concrete poured,
and nail by nail and board by board
Daddy gave life to Mama's dream.

I thought if I could touch this place or feel it
this brokenness inside me might start healing.
Out here its like I'm someone else,
I thought that maybe I could find myself.
If I could just come in I swear I'll leave.
Won't take nothing but a memory
from the house that built me.

You leave home, you move on and you do the best you can.
I got lost in this whole world and forgot who I am.

I thought if I could touch this place or feel it
this brokenness inside me might start healing.
Out here it's like I'm someone else,
I thought that maybe I could find myself.
If I could walk around I swear I'll leave.
Won't take nothing but a memory
from the house that built me.

Acknowledgments

Writing this memoir was an epic journey, and it took an entire team to nourish the creation of this book. I am privileged to have had the dedicated and enthusiastic support of Florence Grace, who spearheaded this project from its very inception, weathering the magical highs and frustrating lows of the writing process with me.

My editor, Christina Roth, and Turner Publishing should be recognized for their bravery in embracing a project they did not start in a publishing landscape that is vastly different from what it was just five years ago when I wrote my first book.

My agent, Steve Troha, deserves major credit for believing in me. I would also like to thank Stephanie Gertler for getting me started on my walk down memory lane. Creating a book of this nature was a learning process. I was fortunate to have Brenda Arechiga, my own personal flashlight along this journey's path.

Of course, I never would have had the courage to sit down and produce this memoir were it not for the influence of Ryan Seacrest and Stuart Krasnow, who together gave me a voice and educated me in the production of reality television. Both Craig Zadan and Neil Meron have not only believed in my talents but also put me on the path to building a life as a single, independent, creative woman, nurturing me to become a successful Broadway producer.

I consider myself fortunate to work with my attorney, Larry Marks. My assistants Jennifer Peterson and Stephanie DeLoach deserve recognition for assembling the complex puzzle of facts necessary to create a time line for the book and also for the patience they show me every day.

Candy Spelling

is the widow of Aaron Spelling, mega-Hollywood producer of hit TV series such as *Dynasty, Charlie's Angels*, and *Beverly Hills 90210*. The *New York Times* bestselling author of *Stories from Candyland*, she is the mother of TV star Tori Spelling, bestselling author of *Spelling It Like It Is, uncharted terriTORI, sTORI telling,* and *Mommywood*. Candy has produced the award-winning Broadway musicals *Promises, Promises, How to Succeed in Business Without Really Trying, Nice Work If You Can Get It,* and *After Midnight*. She appears regularly on national broadcast media including *Good Morning America, Today, The View,* and *The Early Show* and blogs for the Huffington Post and other online media.